Inspired by Og Mandino's
All-Time Best Seller
The Greatest Salesman in the World

The Greatest Sales Training In The World

by
Robert Nelson

*Featuring special
contributions and
comments from
several of the world's
greatest sales and
management training
experts*

The Greatest Sales Training in the World
Frederick Fell Publishers, Inc.
2131 Hollywood Boulevard
Hollywood, Florida 33020
email: fellpub@aol.com

Visit our web site at www.fellpub.com

Library of Congress Cataloging-in-publication Data
Nelson, Robert, 1961–
    The greatest sales training in the world : based on the 10 ancient scrolls of Og Mandino's all-time bestseller, The greatest salesman in the world / by Robert Nelson.
        p.   cm.
    "Commemorative edition"—Prelim. p. [ ].
    Includes bibliographical references and index.
    ISBN 0-88391-121-3 (trade paperback)
    1. Sales personnel—training of. I. Mandino, Og. The greatest salesman in the world.
    II. Title
                       98-37148

**This book is dedicated to the late
great Og Mandino.**

*We are eternally grateful for the legacy
of wisdom that Og gave to the world.
This training program is my attempt to
insure that his immortal truth shall
continue to shine brightly.*

A Special Message from the Publisher

*I*n 1968 Frederick Fell Publishers, Inc. was privileged to publish Og Mandino's *The Greatest Salesman in the World*, the simple story of a salesman who learned the secret of success written on ten ancient scrolls. Since then it has become a classic that has outsold the competition by millions, and it now ranks as the number-one all-time inspiration and sales book ever written.

Out of his personal search for the answers to life's questions, Og discovered secrets to success revealed by some of the greatest minds our world has known. And *The Greatest Salesman in the World* shows you how to use these secrets to empower yourself to live a life of achievement.

When Robert Nelson began his search for a successful salesperson to be his teacher, he picked up a copy of Og Mandino's book and from that moment he became his apprentice.

Now Frederick Fell Publishers, Inc. is proud to present *The Greatest Sales Training in the World* in which Nelson has taken Mandino's principles of the ten ancient scrolls and incorporated them into an inspirational sales training guide that allows you to find success in sales by integrating the same principles of happiness, love, and peace of mind.

In every way, the secrets of the scrolls allow you to become all that you have ever dreamed. All you have to do is read them, read them again, and make them part of your life.

Enjoy!

Most cordially,
Donald L. Lessne
Publisher

Preface

*T*his book was written to commemorate the literary genius Og Mandino, author of the best selling classic *The Greatest Salesman in the World*. For the past 30 years, *The Greatest Salesman in the World* has retained the title as the world's most popular book ever written on the subject of sales. Although Mandino's book is about sales, it does not address the basic sales fundamentals, but does address the ethics and morals that are the foundation of successful salesmanship.

The Greatest Salesman in the World is generally viewed as an inspirational book and is usually found in the religious sections of most bookstores. Unfortunately, the ethical principles expressed in his book are sometimes viewed as separate from what it really takes to achieve sales success. Nothing could be further from the truth. Success in sales and life can only be achieved by discovering and applying the universal principles that Og Mandino so eloquently expressed in the ten scrolls.

The sales profession has developed a bad reputation because salespeople often secure sales through manipulative techniques rather than a sincere desire to serve the customer. As Tom Hopkins, one of America's number one sales trainers, put it, "Some of the world's most persuasive salespeople are in jail." Without moral integrity and a sincere desire to be of service to others, a persuasive salesperson is nothing more than a con-artist. For this reason, I have written this sales-training program: to help you clearly see how the wisdom of the scrolls can be applied effectively to the process of selling to increase your sales profits while maintaining the highest level of moral integrity.

The Greatest Sales Training in the World will reemphasize the indispensable value of Og Mandino's ethical principles. You will learn how the moral value of the ten ancient scrolls can be applied on a practical level to increase sales profits.

Table of Contents

The Sixth Scroll Marked 91

LESSON SIX - EMOTIONAL MASTERY The Two Sides Of Nature - Understanding Mood Swings - The Atmosphere Which Yields Success - Proactive Thought Control - Counteracting Emotional Lows - Counteracting Emotional Highs - Tolerance For Moody People - Immunity To Rejection - Secret Key To Great Wealth - Mastering Moods Skillfully - A Practical Exercise

Charles Jones 102

The Seventh Scroll 109

LESSON SEVEN - SENSE OF HUMOR Laughter Effects Physical Condition - The Ability To Laugh At Yourself - Laughing In The Face Of Adversity - This-Too-Shall-Pass - Stay Too Busy To Be Sad - Laughter Puts Things Into Perspective - The Selfish Use Of Laughter - Exchanging Smiles For Gold - Remaining As A Child - Success Without Happiness - A Practical Exercise

Paul J. Meyer 120

The Eighth Scroll 125

LESSON EIGHT - SELF-IMPROVEMENT Value Multiplied By Genius - The Multipliable Potential In Mankind - Increase Income By Enhancing Output - Nurturing Body And Mind - The Power And Process Of Goal Setting - Setting Yourself Up For A Fall - Surpass Your Own Achievements - Use The Gift Of Prophesy - The Crime Of Mediocrity - Comparing Humans To Plants - A Practical Exercise

Anthony Robbins 138

The Ninth Scroll 147

The Tenth Scroll 167

Introduction

Sales is the starting point of all enterprise and industry. It is one of the highest paid professions in the world, and one of the most feared. Many successful businesses begin with an idea, but it is the selling of this idea that makes them a success.

Regardless of your profession, you will undoubtedly be required to do some form of selling. You may have to sell your boss on giving you that promotion, sell your manager on giving you that assignment, or sell your co-workers on cooperating with your suggestions. Whenever we attempt to persuade someone to see our point of view, we are selling. Therefore, if you can become more skilled in the art of persuasion, you can achieve a greater level of success in whatever you do.

Why is it that some sales people become successful while others become failures? Is it that some are just not "cut out" for sales? Contrary to popular opinion, sales people are not "cut out." There is no special breed simply born to be sales people; sales people are made. Sales is a craft, and just like any other craft, the process can be taught, learned, practiced and eventually mastered.

Although there is no question that effective training plays an important part in the development of a good salesperson, a truly effective sales program is one that increases sales. What you are about to discover is not just another sales training program, but, in fact, The Greatest Sales Training in the World.

Why is this *The Greatest Sales Training in the World?*

First: The information in this program is based upon the "ten ancient scrolls" from Og Mandino's best seller The Greatest Salesman in the World. It will show you how to take the time-tested principles found in Mandino's classic and apply them to your daily life.

Second: This program is guaranteed to help you increase sales profits! Each chapter contains practical exercises that will dramatically enhance your sales ability. You can begin using these strategies immediately to improve your sales results.

In The Beginning

My story begins deep down in the valley of failure. I had what many may consider job security; I was making much more than minimum wage, with the best health and retirement benefits that anyone could ask for. Nevertheless, discontentment drove me from this haven of job security and out into the jungle of entrepreneurship.

Like so many others I was lured by the possibility of an unlimited income and attracted by the freedom of controlling my own time. Independence had seduced me, and, blinded by passion, I had very little knowledge of what it took to maintain this new relationship. I did not have to travel in the darkness of ignorance long to lose my way along the path to success. I became a casualty in the marketplace. As my business venture failed, I was forced to seek employment with another company. Having burned all the bridges that led back to my previous job, I now had to find another open door.

It was here that I first became acquainted with the profession of sales. You see, sales is one profession where there is always an open door. It is like the challenge of riding a wild bronco. So many people jump on the saddle with very little skill and even less awareness of what they are in for. Consequently, they are thrown from the saddle as soon as the ride begins and then develop a great fear of ever reentering the arena. I, too, was painfully thrown from the sales saddle, yet I did not have the option of leaving the sales arena. My only choice was to learn to ride the bronco; I was not content to walk again in the path of failure.

In Search Of A Teacher

To become successful in sales, I began my search for a qualified teacher, most logically a successful salesperson. Unfortunately, most successful salespeople were too busy selling to take time out to provide me with private instruction. My search led me to some of the world's top sales training programs. But because most of these programs were far more expensive than I could afford, I began making small investments in books and audiotapes. I began frequenting the library and found all the sales instruction I needed at no expense.

Such an unlimited flow of sales information became somewhat overwhelming. Although I was swimming in a river of knowledge, I had grown weary and was desperately seeking a place where I could come ashore. Og Mandino's writing proved to be such a place. It is here is that our lesson begins.

After much research I became an apprentice of Og Mandino. My reasoning was simple: the information dealt specifically with sales, the book was easy to read, and the instructions easy to follow. Besides, no one told me that I was not to take this book literally.

At first I was so frightened at the thought of approaching a prospect that I broke out into a cold sweat and trembled nervously as if I were about to faint. After I began learning and applying the principles of the scrolls, the results were nothing less than magical. I went from hiding in the bathroom to confronting thousands of prospects courageously while other sales people sat and watched in awe. My sales techniques were so effective that I felt I could sell a glass of water to a drowning man. In fact, I became so effective I was eventually appointed to the position of director of training and education for The National Black Business Trade Association, responsible for teaching thousands of entrepreneurs how to sell more effectively their products and services. These ancient scrolls have impacted my sales career, and if they can do that for me, they can do the same for you.

Sell or be Sold

One question has been addressed by every sales training program ever created: Is sales for me? The answer is simple: Sales is for you. Every human being is involved in the process of selling. If you don't learn how to sell effectively then you will not be successful.

Consider this fact: Selling is merely the flip side of buying. The average person may not be a professional buyer, but he or she is a consumer. If you don't learn how to be a smart consumer, you will waste money unnecessarily. Likewise, the average person may not be a professional sales person, even though he or she is constantly selling. If you don't learn how to be a smart seller you will be short changed when you trade your products or services.

Buying and selling is to financial survival, what inhaling and exhaling is to physical survival. Just as you cannot survive physically without exhaling, you cannot survive financially without selling. Think about it for a moment. It doesn't matter whether you're a butcher, a baker or a candlestick maker; you are producing some type of service for which you are receiving compensation. The more effective you are at selling what you produce, the more abundant the compensation will be that you receive.

There are people in every profession who sell themselves short, simply because they don't know how to sell themselves. Many work for minimum wage, yet have maximum potential. Others earn far above minimum wage, but are still far below what they are actually worth. These people are being SOLD! They are being sold on believing that their compensation is of equal or greater value to the services they are rendering.

Have you ever felt that you were being paid much less than you are worth? Have you ever seen someone else make much more money for doing much less work than you do? If you answered yes to either of these questions, then you, too, have been selling yourself short. What we will cover in the following lessons will enable you to raise your standards and sell yourself for what you are really worth.

PRE-TRAINING EVALUATION

Before we begin the first lesson, please take the following evaluation. The questions are designed to help you establish a clear picture of where you presently stand in your career. Because this picture will serve as the starting point for your future progress, it is important to be honest in your responses.

After the pre-evaluation, you will proceed with the training. Sixty to ninety days after you have completed the final chapter of this training program, answer the pre-evaluation questions again. This will be your post evaluation. You should notice a distinct difference in your responses because you will have produced measurable results.

Use your memory to answer these questions. Do not refer to notes or any other written material to find the answers. If you don't know an answer to a question, simply leave it blank.

1) What is your profession?

_____

2) What is your company's mission statement?

_____

3) What is your current income? Monthly? Annually?

_____

4) What is your desired income? Monthly? Annually?

_____

5) What single thing can you do to increase your income?

_____

6) What are the opening words of your sales presentation?

_____

7) What is the most important benefit of your product or service?

_____

8) What is the most popular objection to your product or service?

_____

9) How do you usually reply to that objection?

_____

10) What are the most effective words you use to close a sale?

_____

The Legend of the Ten Scrolls

High atop the palace dome, in a room accessible only by a single winding stairway, lay the most precious treasure of Hafid, *The Greatest Salesman in the World.* For over thirty years, two armed guards posted there day and night forbade anyone but Hafid access to this room. Rumors circulated that the room contained barrels of diamonds and gold ingots, or wild animals and rare birds. Some even suggested that the room contained a small harem of exotic beauties kept in secret for Hafid's delight. Yet Hafid proclaimed that even if the room were filled to its beams with diamonds, its value would never compare to the value of what was contained in a simple wooden box, the solitary item in the forbidden room.

Within the box, written on ten ancient scrolls, rested the secret to all the success, happiness, love, peace of mind and wealth which the great salesman had been privileged to enjoy for almost half a century. The box also contained the secret to the wisdom and knowledge directly responsible for his unmatched success. His former employer and mentor, Pathros, had given the scrolls to him. One day Hafid was to pass these scrolls on to someone who could share their enlightening message with the entire world.

Mandino's fable has been shared with millions of readers around the world. Although fiction, these ancient scrolls contain priceless secrets: the keys to wisdom and knowledge that can unlock the door to success and happiness.

Og Mandino has revealed the mysterious secrets behind sales success, yet there are still many that do not understand and apply his wisdom. Now is your chance to take a closer look at this mystery and discover the secrets for yourself.

How to Develop Success Habits

The first scroll is uniquely different from the others. While the nine remaining scrolls teach specific success principles, the first scroll is not a principle; it is a success process.

For example, there are basic rules of the road that we must follow in order to drive a car. If you didn't know how to drive a car, the rules of the road would mean very little to you. Nine of the scrolls are the basic rules that will help you achieve sales success. The first scroll is the actual process you use to drive the car. If you don't understand and apply the process of the first scroll, the remaining nine principles will be of little use.

In the words of Hafid, "The first scroll contains a secret which has been given to a mere handful of wise men throughout history. The first scroll, in truth, teaches the most effective way to learn what is written on the other scrolls."

The scrolls are designed so that the reader can develop rules of conduct, which will ultimately lead to success. The most effective way to develop this conduct is to apply the success process contained in the first scroll so that the remaining nine principles become a standard part of your daily activity.

In truth we are all apprentices. Our behavior and personalities are shaped by the influencing forces that surround us. The key is to choose your own influencing forces, and then expose yourself to these forces regularly so that you can develop the character traits they will produce.

The 1st Scroll Habits

Today I begin a new life. Today I shed my old skin, which hath, too long, suffered the bruises of failure and the wounds of mediocrity.

Today I am born anew and my birthplace is a vineyard where there is fruit for all.

Today I will pluck grapes of wisdom from the tallest and fullest vines in the vineyard, for these were planted by the wisest of my profession who have come before me, generation upon generation.

Today I will savor the taste of grapes from these vines and verily I will swallow the seed of success buried in each and new life will sprout within me.

The career I have chosen is laden with opportunity yet it is fraught with heartbreak and despair and the bodies of those who have failed, were they piled one atop another, would cast a shadow down upon all the pyramids of the earth.

Yet I will not fail, as the others, for in my hands I now hold the charts, which will guide me through perilous waters to shores, which only yesterday seemed but a dream.

Failure no longer will be my payment for struggle. Just as nature made no provision for my body to tolerate pain neither has it made any provision for my life to suffer failure. Failure, like pain, is alien to my life. In the past I accepted it as I accepted pain. Now I reject it and I am prepared for wisdom and principles which will guide me out of the shadows into the sunlight of wealth, position, and happiness far beyond my most extravagant dreams until even the golden apples in the Garden of Hesperides will seem no more than my just reward.

Time teaches all things to he who lives forever but I have not the luxury of eternity. Yet, within my allotted time I must practice the art of patience for nature acts never in haste. To create the olive, king of all trees, a hundred years is required. An onion plant is old in nine weeks. I have lived as an onion plant. It has not pleased me. Now I wouldst become the greatest of olive trees and, in truth, the greatest of salesmen.

And how will this be accomplished? For I have neither the knowledge nor the experience to achieve greatness and already I have stumbled in ignorance and fallen into pools of self-pity. The answer is simple. I will commence my journey unencumbered with either the weight of unnecessary knowledge or the handicap of meaningless experience. **Nature already has supplied me with knowledge and instinct far greater than any beast** in the forest and the value of experience is overrated, usually by old men who nod wisely and speak stupidly.

In truth, experience teaches thoroughly yet her course of instruction devours men's years so the value of her lessons diminishes with the time necessary to acquire her special wisdom. The end finds it wasted on dead men. Furthermore, experience is comparable to fashion; an action that proved successful today will be unworkable and impractical tomorrow.

Only principles endure and these I now possess, for the laws that will lead me to greatness are contained in the words of these scrolls. What they will teach me is more to prevent failure than to gain success, for what is success other than a state of mind?

Which two, among a thousand wise men, will define success in the same words; yet failure is always described but one way. Failure is man's inability to reach his goals in life, whatever they may be.

In truth, **the only difference between those who have failed and those who have succeeded lies in the difference of their habits.** Good habits are the key to all success. Bad habits are the unlocked door to failure. Thus, the first law I will obey, which precedeth all others is—I will form good habits and become their slave.

As a child I was slave to my impulses; now I am slave to my habits, as are all grown men. I have surrendered my free will to the years of accumulated habits and the past deeds of my life have already marked out a path, which threatens to imprison my future. My actions are ruled by appetite, passion, prejudice, greed, love, fear, environment, habit, and the worst of these tyrants is habit. Therefore, if I must be a slave to habit let me be a slave to good habits. My bad habits must be destroyed and new furrows prepared for good seed.

I will form good habits and become their slave.

And how will I accomplish this difficult feat? Through these scrolls, it will be done, for each scroll contains a principle which will drive a bad habit from my life and replace it with one which will bring me closer to success. For **it is another of nature's laws that only a habit can subdue another habit**. So, in order for these written words to perform their chosen task, I must discipline myself with the first of my new habits which is as follows: I will read each scroll for thirty days in this prescribed manner, before I proceed to the next scroll.

First, I will read the words in silence when I arise. Then, I will read the words in silence after I have partaken of my midday meal. Last, I will read the words again just before I retire at day's end, and most important, on this occasion I will read the words aloud.

On the next day I will repeat this procedure, and I will continue in like manner for thirty days. Then, I will turn to the next scroll and repeat this procedure for another thirty days. I will continue in this manner until I have lived with each scroll for thirty days and my reading has become habit.

And what will be accomplished with this habit? **Herein lies the**

hidden secret of all man's accomplishments. As I repeat the words daily they will soon become a part of my active mind, but more important, they will also seep into my other mind, that mysterious source which never sleeps, which creates my dreams, and often makes me act in ways I do not comprehend.

As the words of these scrolls are consumed by my mysterious mind I will begin to awake, each morning, with vitality I have never known before. My vigor will increase, my enthusiasm will rise, my desire to meet the world will overcome every fear I once knew at sunrise, and I will be happier than I ever believed it possible to be in this world of strife and sorrow.

Eventually I will find myself reacting to all situations which confront me as I was commanded in the scrolls to react, and soon these actions and reactions will become easy to perform, for any act with practice becomes easy.

Thus a new and good habit is born, **for when an act becomes easy through constant repetition it becomes a pleasure to perform and if it is a pleasure to perform it is man's nature to perform it often. When I perform it often it becomes a habit and I become its slave and since it is a good habit this is my will.**

Today I begin a new life.

And I make a solemn oath to myself that nothing will retard my new life's growth. I will lose not a day from these readings for that day cannot be retrieved nor can I substitute another for it. **I must not, I will not, break this habit** of daily reading from these scrolls and, in truth, the few moments spent each day on this new habit are but a small price to pay for the happiness and success that will be mine.

As I read and re-read the words in the scrolls to follow, never will I allow the brevity of each scroll or the simplicity of its words to cause me to treat the scroll's message lightly. Thousands of grapes are pressed to fill one jar with wine, and the grapeskin and pulp are tossed to the birds. So it is with these grapes of wisdom from the ages. Much has been filtered and tossed to the wind. Only the pure truth lies distilled in the words to come. I will drink as instructed and spill not a drop. And the seed of success I will swallow.

Today my old skin has become as dust. **I will walk tall among men and they will know me not, for today I am a new man, with a new life.**

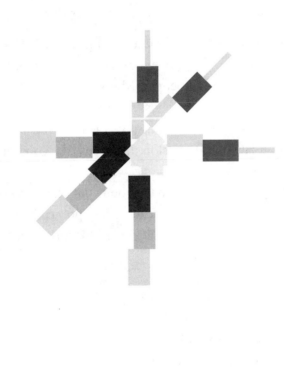

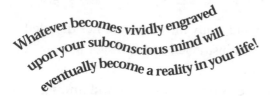

Whatever becomes vividly engraved upon your subconscious mind will eventually become a reality in your life!

Success Habits
T h e   1 s t   L e s s o n

In Dr. Stephen R. Covey's best selling book, *7 Habits of Highly Effective People*, Dr. Covey describes seven personality traits inherent in highly effective people. Many books point out these same qualities, which we need to possess if we truly want to become successful. The first scroll is perhaps the clearest and simplest explanation. It tells you HOW TO develop the necessary good habits that will lead to success.

The first scroll reveals how to use the ritual of spaced repetition that will shape your behavior. The following key points from the first scroll will help you understand how to apply this principle effectively to create the habits that you desire.

1 | Starting Fresh
"Today I begin a new life"

The first step in developing successful sales habits is to decide that you will make a fresh start. Although this is the most important step, it is usually the most difficult. In order to start fresh you must first realize that some of your old habits are not taking you in the direction you want.

Yet, before you can begin developing new habits, you must first identify and acknowledge your negative habits. Only then can you begin the process of self-improvement that will mold you into the person you want to be.

2 | Choose Opportunity or Despair
"The career I have chosen is laden with opportunity yet it is fraught with heartbreak and despair..."

Regardless of what situations occur in life, the way you respond determines the ultimate outcome. If you make a conscious effort to look at the opportunity, which exists in every opposition, your optimism will enable you to create the outcome you desire.

3 | Work With What You Have
"Nature already has supplied me with knowledge and instinct far greater than any beast in the forest..."

If we see ourselves lacking in certain skills, knowledge, or ability, we will act inferior to those who do possess such qualities.

The truth is that most people are endowed at birth with enough wit and common sense to achieve a certain level of success. Our education is designed to teach us how to use these tools, and the challenges of life provide us with opportunities to practice and improve these skills. If we face these challenges aware that we are already equipped with most of the tools needed to achieve success, then we are able to create more successful results. Taking inventory of the natural qualities you possess will help you build the confidence it takes to achieve success.

4 | Difference Between Success and Failure

"The only difference between those who have failed and those who have succeeded lies in the difference of their habits."

The key difference between a success and a failure is that successful people habitually do things that lead to success while failures do not.

If the key difference between success and failure lies in the habits they possess, doesn't it seem wise to observe the habits of successful people and to develop those habits as a standard part of your daily life? Before you begin developing your new set of habits, let us take a look at a simple process you can use to remove undesirable habits.

5 | Substituting vs. Omitting Habits

"It is another of nature's laws that only a habit can subdue another habit."

Don't say: "I am going to stop being late for meetings." Do say and believe: "I am going to stop being late for meetings and start being early." Don't say: "I am going to start making more sales calls." Do say and believe: "I am going to start making more sales calls and stop watching so much TV." Although it will take some time to develop good habits, the process will be easier and the results will last longer if you use the substitution method.

6 | The Power of Spaced Repetition

"First, I will read the words in silence when I arise. Then, I will read the words in silence after I have partaken of my midday meal. Last, I will read the words again just before I

retire at the day's end, and most important, on this occasion I will read the words aloud."

There are many effective memory programs today, yet the oldest and most frequently used process is spaced repetition. It is through spaced repetition that we digest information and make it a permanent part of our memory, just as we learned our ABCs as a child or the lyrics to songs.

In his lectures on "Seeds of Greatness," Dr. Denis Waitley explains that through the "reticular activating system" our brains determine which things we will be consciously aware of and which things we will consciously ignore. By using spaced repetition we can force our reticular activating system to be consciously aware of the information and ideas that we have specifically selected to help us reach our goal of success.

7 | Programming your Hard Drive
"Herein lies the hidden secret of all man's accomplishments. As I repeat the words daily they will soon become a part of my active mind, but more important, they will also seep into my other mind,..."

The computer was designed to operate like the human mind. Amazingly, there are many people who understand how computers work, yet still have trouble understanding how the mind works. There are two forms of memory within both the computer and the human mind: temporary memory and permanent memory.

In a computer the temporary memory is called RAM (Random Access Memory). This memory projects the images we see on the screen. The permanent memory is called the hard drive and this is where the vast stockpile of information is stored.

The short-term memory, or conscious part of the human mind, is like the RAM. This is what we use to retain information temporarily—a phone number we need to dial or what we ordered for lunch. The long-term memory, or subconscious part of the human mind, is like the computer's hard drive. This is our vast storehouse of information and it is here that we keep the programmed habits that run our lives.

In order to develop the habits that will lead us to success, we must first program these habits into our sub-conscious minds. The things we hear, see, and experience over and over are the things that penetrate our conscious minds and seep deep down in to our sub-conscious minds. These are the things that effect our behavior, beliefs, and ultimately, our destiny.

8 | Steps to Building Habits

"...when an act becomes easy through constant repetition it becomes a pleasure to perform, and if it is a pleasure to perform, it is man's nature to perform it often. When I perform it often it becomes a habit and I become it's slave and, since this is a good habit, this is my will."

Developing a new habit involves three phases. The process involves repeating an action that you wish to become a habit and repeating it often, until it becomes part of your nature. During the first phase you may experience some initial discomfort. This is an exercise of the mind, and, like any other form of exercise, may seem like hard work. Don't let this discourage you; instead, let it serve as encouragement. Continue to repeat the action and let the presence of discomfort serve as an indication that you are on the right track.

Soon the discomfort will begin to diminish, and you will find the process becoming easier. You have now entered the second phase. At this point you may think your work is done; however, you have not yet mastered the habit itself, and if you do not continue repeating the action, you may fall back into your old habits.

You'll know you have reached the third and final phase when repeating the action becomes a pleasure. In fact, you may begin to crave it, like chocolate or junk food. At this point the habit will begin to influence your subconscious actions, and you will perform the action even when you are not thinking about it. Your habit is on automatic pilot, so to speak, and it is now part of you.

9 | Commitment to Build Daily
"I must not, I will not, break this habit..."

While you are working to develop a particular habit, you must make a personal commitment to stick with it until it has been completed. Even when you neglect to follow through, you must start over until you get it done. The integrity of your word to yourself is sacred. By making constant commitments to yourself, and striving to follow through, you will build a habit of personal integrity.

10 | Becoming a New Person
"I will walk tall among men and they will not know me for today I am a new man, with a new life."

Your new behavior may seem strange to your friends, family, and associates. Some may even try to persuade you to stop trying to be something they think you are not. Don't let them sell you on this idea. People you know who possess habits you want to develop will encourage your new conduct and motivate you to continue striving for personal improvement. Those who do not possess these habits may become offended at your desire to be different. Therefore, try to surround yourself with those who will support your desire for positive change.

❗ Developing Habit: A Practical Exercise
Developing a Definite Chief Aim: The most common habit among successful people

The single most important step to success is to determine exactly where you want to go. Success means different things to different people. Therefore, you must develop a crystal clear picture of your success so that you will recognize it when you reach it. The first scroll will help you focus your mind on what you want to achieve in the nine different areas of your life, which are addressed in the remaining scrolls.

In the words of Napoleon Hill, "The method by which desire for riches can be transmuted into its financial equivalent consists of six definite, practical steps."

First: Fix in your mind the exact amount of money you desire. It is not sufficient merely to say, "I want plenty of money." Be definite as to the amount.

Second: Determine exactly what you intend to give in return for the money.

Third: Establish a definite date for when you intend to possess the money.

Fourth: Create a definite plan for carrying out your desire, and begin at once, whether you are ready or not, to put this plan into action.

Fifth: Write out a clear, concise statement of the amount of money, name the time limit for its acquisition, state what you intend to give in return for the money, and describe clearly the plan through which you intend to accumulate it.

Sixth: Read your written statement three times daily: once when you arise, once after your midday meal, and once aloud just before retiring. As you read, try to visualize yourself already in possession of the money."

Conduct this exercise for 30 days, or until you have completely memorized your definite chief aim. This exercise applies the principle of the first scroll in a practical way that can directly impact your sales profits and/or personal income.

S p o t l i g h t   o n :

Les Brown

Author • Sales Trainer

In 1989, Les Brown was the recipient of the National Speakers Association's highest honor: The Council of Peers Award of Excellence (CAPE). In addition, he was selected as one of the world's top five speakers for 1992, by Toastmasters International, and recipient of the Golden Gavel Award.

As a renowned professional speaker, author and television personality, Les Brown has risen to national prominence by delivering a high energy message which tells people how to shake off mediocrity and live up to their greatness. It is a message Les Brown has learned from his own life and one he is helping others apply to their lives.

Born in low-income Liberty City, in Miami, Florida, Les and his twin brother, Wes, were adopted when they were six weeks old by Mrs. Mamie Brown. Mrs. Brown was a single woman who had very little education or financial means, but a very big heart. As a child Les' inattention to school work, his restless energy, and the failure of his teachers to recognize his true potential resulted in him being mislabeled as a slow learner. The label and the stigma stayed with him, damaging his self-esteem to such an extent that it took several years to overcome.

Although Les has had no formal education beyond high school,

through persistence and determination he has initiated and continued a process of unending self education which has distinguished him as an authority on harnessing human potential. Les Brown's passion to learn and his hunger to realize greatness in himself and others allowed him to achieve greatness. He rose from a hip-talking morning DJ to broadcast manager; from community activist to community leader; from political commentator to three-term legislator; and from a banquet and nightclub emcee to premier keynote speaker. In 1986, Les entered the public speaking arena on a full-time basis and formed his own company, Les Brown Enterprises, Inc. The company provides motivational tapes and materials, workshops, and personal/professional development programs aimed at individual, companies, and organizations.

In 1990, Les recorded his first in a series of speech presentations entitled You Deserve, which was awarded a Chicago-area Emmy, and became a leading fund-raising program of its kind for pledges to PBS stations nationwide.

Les Brown is now an internationally recognized speaker and CEO of Les Brown Enterprises, Inc.; he is also the author of the highly acclaimed and successful books, *Live Your Dreams*, and a newly released book, *It's Not Over Until You Win*. As the former host of The Les Brown Show, a nationally syndicated daily television talk show focusing on solutions, rather than problems, Les Brown aptly fits his reputation as one of the nation's leading authorities in understanding and stimulating human potential. Utilizing powerful delivery and newly emerging insights, Les' customized presentations teach, inspire, and channel audiences to new levels of achievement.

! • | Discovering the Secrets of the Successful

How did you get started in the field of sales?
I started out at age nine selling new and used television sets door to door.

What is the greatest challenge you have had to face over the years?
The greatest challenge is constantly selling myself on the fact that it was possible I could live my dream, and that I could have the things I desired in life.

What do you consider to be the most outstanding achievement of your career?
I would say the most outstanding achievement was coming to a place within myself that I realized you don't get in life what you want, you get in life what you are. I have come to be that kind of person. All of those the things I've set out to achieve I've done those things all in myself.

Who were some of you most influential role models and mentors?
My mother who adopted seven kids and Mr. Leroy Washington, a high school teacher. After I had been labeled as mentally retarded I was put back from the fifth to the fourth grade. For a while I too came to believe that I was mentally handicapped. Then in the eleventh grade I met Mr. Washington who impacted my life tremendously. He taught me never to let someone else's opinion of me become my reality.

What is the most effective sales technique you have ever used?
I would say that the most effective sales technique I have ever used is adopting the mind set when you make eye contact with a customer that the deal is closed and it's a done deal. That look in your eyes is the only reason they were spared from birth control.

Give an example of how you would apply this technique in a real life situation?

Whatever you're confronted with you must allow your doubt to starve to death. You must have absolute faith, conditioned faith.

What is the most valuable advice you can offer an aspiring sales person?

Number one, engage in an ongoing process of working at loving yourself.

If you have not always lived by your current philosophy, what provoked the change?

The feeling that I had within myself that there had to be more to life than I was experiencing.

Ten Ancient Scrolls
Les Brown

*T*eaching people how to experience their greatest is my business. Og Mandino's *The Greatest Salesman in the World* has always inspired me and is one of the most dependable and accurate descriptions of the process of how to live our dreams and achieve the success we all seek. Og's special magic directs us in how to apply these principles each day of our lives.

I started out in door to door sales at age nine. One day, someone gave me the book, *The Greatest Salesman in the World*, and more than any other book, it impacted my life unbelievably! I would sleep with it under my pillow. I practiced and read the scrolls daily as Og instructed, and my sales went through the roof and my life was never the same. What a blessing he was for the planet and for all who have had the good fortune to read his life-changing book. We are so fortunate that God selected Og to be the vessel for this great book that will change the lives of generations yet unborn.

The 2nd Scroll: Love

I will greet this day with love in my heart.

For this is the greatest secret of success in all ventures. Muscle can split a shield and even destroy life but only the unseen power of love can open the hearts of men and until I master this art I will remain no more than a peddler in the market place. **I will make love my greatest weapon and none on which I call can defend against its force.**

My reasoning they may counter; my speech they may distrust; my apparel they may disapprove; my face they may reject; and even my bargains may cause them suspicion; yet my love will melt all hearts liken to the sun whose rays soften the coldest clay.

I will greet this day with love in my heart.

And how will I do this? **Henceforth will I look on all things with love** and I will be born again. I will love the sun for it warms my bones; yet I will love the rain for it cleanses my spirit. I will love the light for it shows me the way; yet I will love the darkness for it shows me the stars. I will welcome happiness for it enlarges my heart; yet I will endure sadness for it opens my soul. I will acknowledge rewards for they are my due; yet I will welcome obstacles for they are my challenge.

I will greet this day with love in my heart.

And how will I speak? **I will laud mine enemies and they will become friends;** I will encourage my friends and they will become brothers. Always will I dig for reasons to applaud; never will I scratch for excuses to gossip. When I am tempted to criticize I will bite on my tongue; when I am moved to praise I will shout from the roofs.

Is it not so that birds, the wind, the sea and all nature speaks with the music of praise for their creator? Cannot I speak with the same music to his children? Henceforth will I remember this secret and it will change my life.

I will greet this day with love in my heart.

And how will I act? **I will love all manners of men for each has qualities to be admired even though they be hidden.** With love I will tear down the wall of suspicion and hate which they have built round their hearts and in its place will I build bridges so that my love may enter their souls.

I will love the ambitious for they can inspire me! I will love the failures for they can teach me. I will love the kings for they are but human; I will love the meek for they are divine. I will love the rich for they are yet lonely; I will love the poor for they are so many. I will love the young for the faith they hold; I will love the old for the wisdom they share. I will love the beautiful for their eyes of sadness; I will love the ugly for their souls of peace.

I will greet this day with love in my heart.

But how will I react to the actions of others? With love. **For just as love is my weapon to open the hearts of men, love is also my shield to repulse the arrows of hate and the spears of anger.** Adversity and discouragement will beat against my new shield and become as the softest of rains. My shield will protect me in the market place and sustain me when I am alone. It will uplift me in moments of despair yet it will calm me in time of exultation. It will become stronger and more protective with use until one day I will cast it aside and walk unencumbered among all manners of men and, when I do, my name will be raised high on the pyramid of life.

I will greet this day with love in my heart.

And how will I confront each whom I meet? In only one way. In silence and to myself I will address him and say I Love You. Though spoken in silence these words will shine in my eyes, unwrinkle my brow, bring a smile to my lips, and echo in my voice; and his heart will be opened. And who is there who will say nay to my goods when his heart feels my love?

I will greet this day with love in my heart.

And most of all I will love myself. For when I do I will zealously inspect all things which enter my body, my mind, my soul, and my heart. Never will I overindulge the requests of my flesh; rather I will cherish my body with cleanliness and moderation. Never will I allow my mind to be attracted to evil and despair, rather I will uplift it with the knowledge and wisdom of the ages. Never will I allow my soul to become complacent and satisfied, rather I will feed it with meditation and prayer. Never will I allow my heart to become small and bitter, rather I will share it and it will grow and warm the earth.

I will greet this day with love in my heart.

Henceforth will I love all mankind. **From this moment all hate is let from my veins** for I have not time to hate, only time to love. From this moment I take the first step required to become a man among men. With love I will increase my sales a hundredfold and become a great salesman. **If I have no other qualities I can succeed with love alone.** Without it I will fail though I possess all the knowledge and skills of the world. I will greet this day with love, and I will succeed.

People Skills
The 2nd Lesson

Whatever becomes vividly engraved upon your subconscious mind will eventually become a reality in your life!

*L*ove is the first of nine success principles revealed in the ten scrolls. It is first because none of the other principles can be applied effectively unless your motivation is based on love. You must have love for your profession, love for the people around you, love for yourself. Love can be developed if you apply it to your daily life.

More than any other profession, sales is a people-centered business. Therefore, effective people skills are the most important tools that a salesperson can have. Love is the fundamental basis for the development of the people skills required to achieve sales success.

The second scroll reveals how to develop a sales attitude that will enable you to persuade prospects masterfully and obtain more sales. Love is the foundation of all pleasant relationships, and a pleasant relationship is the best starting point for a successful sale. The following key points will help you identify areas where love can help you increase your sales profits.

1| Love as an Offensive Weapon
"I will make love my greatest weapon."

Love is the most effective weapon for conquering opposition.

When conflict exists, the aim should be to resolve it. All too often we conclude that the way to resolve the conflict is to destroy the other person. This negative reaction is as senseless as destroying a stained garment. The aim should be to remove the stain, not destroy the garment. Likewise, the aim of every sales encounter should be to gain cooperation from the prospect, not destroy the sales opportunity.

Abraham Lincoln had enemies who sought to slander his name and ruin his public image. He learned to respond by being polite and hospitable. When he was instructed by an advisor to retaliate against his enemies, he responded with the wise words, "Do I not destroy my enemies when I make them my friends?"

2| The Consumer Defense System
"None on whom I call can defend against its force."

Everyday consumers are bombarded with advertisements. It's no wonder that as soon as they sense the presence of a salesperson, they immediately become defensive and do all they can to keep him away from their money.

When your prospects begin to hunt for excuses and try desperately to avoid making a commitment to buy, realize that it's merely an instinctive reaction. Don't take it personally. Once these same prospects begin to sense your genuine concern, all their defenses will start to come down.

The wise salesperson knows that the defense system of consumers must be penetrated. Love is perhaps the world's most effective tool for breaking through the resistance.

3 | The Art of Spotting Hidden Benefits
"Henceforth will I look on all things with love and I will be born again."

As Napoleon Hill, one of the world's foremost authorities on the subject of success, said, "In every adversity there is the seed of an equivalent benefit." From carefully analyzing over 500 of the most successful people of his time, Mr. Hill discovered that one of the things they all held in common was relentless optimism. The ability to look at any situation and find the benefit it holds should be a reflex action of the successful sales person.

4 | Persuasive Power of Praise
"I will laud mine enemies and they will become friends; I will encourage my friends and they will become brothers."

Words have the power to sooth or to irritate. Whenever you use praise to highlight the good qualities in most people, you are giving them something they enjoy hearing. As a result, they become more inclined to cooperate with a request.

5 | Embracing and Valuing Diversity
"I will love all manners of men for each has qualities to be admired even though they be hidden."

If everyone on the planet were alike, the world would be a boring place. Variety is the spice of life. Differences in people and experiences are what make life interesting. So, we must appreciate the fact that each person contributes something unique.

Once we begin identifying positive qualities in others, we will stop seeing the negative ways in which they differ from us. Developing the habit of acknowledging their unique attributes will enable us to develop a greater love for humanity.

Developing your capacity to appreciate diversity will also enhance your ability to highlight the unique selling points of your product or service. When you find prospects who object to your goods because they differ from others in the marketplace, you can emphasize that difference as the key reason why they should buy your product or services. If you value your diversity, others will, too.

6 | Love as a Defensive Weapon
"For just as love is my weapon to open the hearts of men, love is also my shield to repulse the arrows of hate and the spears of anger."

Just as love can be an offensive weapon to transform others into friends, love also can be a defensive weapon to keep others from transforming you into the enemy. And by guarding your heart with love you can keep it from becoming contaminated by bitterness and resentment.

We may not be able to control other people's actions, but we can control our reactions. If you use love to protect yourself from the negative actions, your reaction will produce positive results.

7 | The Confrontational Attitudes
"And how will I confront each whom I meet."

For many people, one of the most frightening things in the world is meeting new people. For this reason, the cold call is the most feared of all prospecting methods. Approaching the people you meet with an attitude of love will allow you to disarm their defenses and make a positive first impression.

8 | Wholesome Self-Love
"And most of all I will love myself."

There is a fine line between wholesome self-appreciation, and self-centered egotistical conceit. Nothing will drive people away faster than a conceited person. And although someone with low self-esteem may not run others away, he or she would not draw people closer.

Because sales is a people-oriented business, many salespeople neglect to cultivate a healthy self-love. While putting the customer first is noble, you don't have to leave yourself out of the picture altogether. You cannot have a genuine love for others unless you first have some degree of love for yourself.

Taking proper care of yourself will help you better serve your customers. YOU are still the single most important sales tool that you will ever possess. Therefore, feed your body and mind a healthy diet of nutritional food and positive information. Maintain an optimistic attitude and a powerful spirit, and your self-love will inspire others to love you as well.

9 | Identify and Dismiss Hates
"From this moment all hate is let from my veins for I have not time to hate, only time to love."

We probably all hate something. However, when we harbor hatred toward others, it tends to do more damage to the hater than it does to the person being hated.

Hatred is one of the waste products of life, and it should be cleansed from our emotional system just as waste is cleansed from our physical system.

10 | Love vs. Knowledge and Skill
"If I have no other qualities I can succeed with love alone. Without it I will fail though I possess all the knowledge and skills of the world."

People do not care how much you know, but they do know how much you care. If you had so much knowledge and skill in sales that you could sell the deed to the world and everything in it, your success could still be shallow and unfulfilling. Yet, if you had so little knowledge and skill that you could not even sell one seamless robe, you could still end up becoming the greatest salesperson in the world.

Love for yourself, other people, and your product or service are important ingredients for achieving sales success. And, if you take that love and combine it with knowledge and skill, you will become a sales success.

! | Developing Love: A Practical Exercise

Sincere love for what you do and the people you serve is the most persuasive sales technique in the world. As a salesperson you will encounter all types of people and not all of them will be loveable. Nevertheless, before I show you how to strengthen your love muscle, let us make sure that we are building on a solid foundation.

One of the most important rules of sales is this: To become a successful salesperson you must first be sold on what you are selling. Do you love what you do and are you convinced that your product, service or profession is of great value to the people you are serving?

Choosing a career is as important as choosing a mate. Often people get involved in a profession or business venture for the wrong reasons, just like people sometimes get married for the wrong reasons. The opportunity may seem attractive, and the potential for making a huge sum of money may seem irresistible. However, if you enter into a relationship strictly for looks or money, and without love as your basic motivation, chances are the relationship will not last. A professional relationship, just like a marriage, should be established on the basis of love in order to endure the many tests that time will bring.

It does not matter if you love your work now. Don't quit your present position and move on to another until you have applied what you will learn here and have sincerely tried to make your current professional relationship work. If you apply these principles, you can turn even a dead-end job into a labor of love.

Answering the following questions can help you identify your labor of love.

What type of work do you enjoy the most?

_____

What type of work have you been told that you do very well?

_____

What type of work would you do if you were guaranteed to succeed?

_____

What type of work do you enjoy in your spare time?

_____

What type of work do you find yourself talking about frequently?

_____

What type of work does the person whom you most admire do?

_____

What type of work would you do if you only had three years to live?

_____

What profession would you be willing to have inscribed on your tombstone?

_____

Honest answers to these questions will help you identify your labor of love. You may notice that one type of work appears frequently as a response. If that response is different from the type of work you do, you may want to consider a career change. However, before you do, use the following exercise to see if you can transform your present profession into a labor of love.

For the next thirty days, if you perform this exercise, your capacity for love will increase. Search for one positive quality in every person you meet and comment on it in a sincere manner. Also, refrain from commenting on any negative qualities, even though they may be painfully obvious. Approach this exercise as a serious experiment; you will be amazed at the magical impact it has on you and everyone you meet.

SELFLESS LOVE

For love of beauty the flower is cut at the stem and placed in a vase where it withers and dies. For love of grace a bird is caught and placed in a cage where it can no longer fly. Selfish love seeks its own gratification with no regard for the best interest of the object of its affection. Unselfish love would free the bird and leave the flower uncut so that their beauty and grace could remain undamaged. Likewise, the love in the heart of a truly great salesperson must be unselfish in nature.

The love you have for your product, your customers and your profession must be selfless. Love not your customer as a lion loves to stalk and catch its prey; rather love them as a mother loves to care for the needs of her children. Love not your product as a robber loves his gun; rather love your product as a doctor loves the bandage used to bind the wound of a patient. Though rewards from sales can indeed be great, seeking the reward is like reaching your hand into a stream to capture the water; the harder you try to clutch the elusive substance, the faster it escapes your grasp.

If you have nothing to sell that will in any way enrich the world, then sell nothing. If the task you perform to obtain your daily bread does not benefit mankind, then stop immediately. However, if you have a product or service that could enhance the life of one person in even the smallest way, then stand courageously and proclaim it boldly throughout the world. Be enthusiastic about what you have, and make it known to the world as if you hold the cure to a terminal illness.

S p o t l i g h t   o n :

Ken Blanchard

Speaker • Co Author of The One Minute Manager

Ken's impact as a writer is far reaching. His best-selling book *The One Minute Manager*, co-authored with Spencer Johnson, has sold more than nine million copies worldwide and is still on best-seller lists. *The One Minute Manager* has been translated into more than 25 languages and is regarded as one of the most successful business books of all time.

In addition, Dr. Blanchard has written several other successful books, including five more within The One Minute Manager Library. He co-authored *The Power of Ethical Management* with Dr. Norman Vincent Peale. In 1992, he released *Playing the Great Game of Golf*, followed by *Raving Fans: A Revolutionary Approach to Customer Service*, co-authored with Sheldon Bowles. In 1994 Ken released *We Are the Beloved*, a book about his spiritual journey, and 1995 released the best-seller *Everyone's a Coach*, co-authored with Don Shula, former head coach of the Miami Dolphins. In 1996 Ken released *Empowerment Takes More Than a Minute* with Alan Randolph and John Carlos, *Managing by Values* with Michael O'Connor, and *Mission Possible: Creating a World Class Organization* with Terry Waghorn. His latest book *Gung Ho!* co-authored with Sheldon Bowles, is

currently climbing the best-seller charts.

Dr. Blanchard is chief spiritual officer of The Ken Blanchard Companies, Inc., a full-service, global management training and consulting company that he and his wife, Dr. Marjorie Blanchard, founded in 1979 in San Diego, California. He is also visiting lecturer at his alma mater, Cornell University, where he is a trustee emeritus of the Board of Trustees.

Dr. Blanchard has received several awards and honors for his contributions in the field of management, leadership, and speaking. In 1991 the National Speakers Association awarded him its highest honor, the "Council of Peers Award of Excellence." In 1992 Dr. Blanchard was inducted into the HRD Hall of Fame by Training Magazine and Lakewood Conferences, and he also received the 1992 Golden Gavel Award from Toastmasters International. In 1996, Ken received the Distinguished Contribution to Human Resource Development Award from the American society of Training and Development.

! • | Discovering the Secrets of the Successful

How did you get started in the field of sales?
It was my intention to go into sales. I took a Kuder preference test in high school and it said I would be a perfect salesman. So I thought I'd go to a good Ivy League school, get a gentleman's 75 average, and present my body to the biggest and best company for a career in sales.

In 1960 during my junior year in college, I was a finalist for a top summer sale program for college students. Twenty finalists were brought in from all over the country to New York to pick the twelve who would be in the program. I didn't make the cut. I couldn't believe it. I wrote the vice president of personnel and said, obviously he made a mistake. I could outsell any of the people he chose. People who knew him said he never got that kind of letter from a college student. But as the result I kissed off the sales field in general and decided to pursue other avenues. I agree with John Lennon who said "Life is what happens to you when you arc planning on doing something else." By various means I ended up being a college professor. In a period of 10 years I rose up the academic ladder to become a tenured full professor at the University of Massachusetts teaching leadership and organizational behavior. In 1976 I went on sabbatical leave to California for one year and never came back. We ran into an entrepreneurial group called The Young Presidents Organization (YPO) and they convinced Marge and me that we should start our own company. The Ken Blanchard Companies is the result. We have about 240 people working with us in the United States and partners in thirty nations. We are a full service management training and consulting company.

What's the greatest challenge you have had to face over the years?
The same challenge that everyone faces—my ego. EGO stands for Edging God Out. When this occurs, you put yourself in the center of everything, and your life is run by fear. Fear of rejection, fear of loosing power, fear of loosing affection, fear of change. When your ego's in

charge you are always asking, "What is in my best interest?" If you can get your ego out of the way, you are asking, "How can I best serve." Every day my ego pops up ready to steer me in the wrong direction. Combating my ego is a one day at a time process.

What do you consider the most outstanding achievement of your career?

Undoubtedly the incredible sales of my book, *The One Minute Manager* is the most outstanding achievement of my career. It was on the New York Times Best Seller List for three years, and now some 17 years later it made the July Wall Street Journal, Business Best Seller List. The book is still selling over 10,000 copies a month.

Who were some of your most influential role models and mentors?

The two biggest had to be my mom and dad. My dad was an Admiral in the Navy and a wonderful model for Servant Leadership. He had his "underdog" and thought his job was to help facilitate his people to becoming the best that they could be. My mother was a walking values recording. She was teaching all of the time. The biggest thing I learned from her was, "Don't let anybody act like they are better than you, but don't act like you're better than anybody else. You all are children of God."

   Norman Vincent Peale has also had a tremendous impact on me. I met him when he was 86 years old and wrote *The Power of Ethical Management* with him. I never met anyone quite like Norman Vincent Peale. It didn't matter if you were a stranger or a long lost friend, when he focused on you; you were the most important person in the world. I never saw him looking around the room to see if there was anybody more important to talk to, or wondering about the next phone call. Once you were in his sight, you were the center of his attention. What a wonderful model of true pride.

What is the most effective sales technique you have ever used?

Making people Raving Fan Customers. A Raving Fan Customer is someone who is so excited about working with you that they want to brag about you. They become part of your sales force. When your goal is to create Raving Fan Customers, all your emphasis is on serving their interests the best way that you can.

Give an example of how you would apply this technique in a real situation?
Every time I talk to a customer, I am asking myself, "How can I create a story out of this interaction? What can I do to exceed this person's expectations?" Story generation is what makes Raving Fan Customers. This involves going the extra mile, rather than quacking like a duck, telling a person about your policies, you soar like an eagle saying, "It will be done."

What is the most valuable advice you can offer an inspiring sales person?
Remember that spiritual significance is more important than earthly success. Earthly success evolves pushing and shoving for money, achievement, and power. While those are not bad things in and of themselves, they become a problem when you identify who you are by those things. I see too many sales people doing that.

Spiritual significance involves generosity, besides wealth, serving others besides achieving, and having loving relationships besides power and status. If you will focus on being a generous, loving, serving person, I think you'll be amazed how well you will do in the sales field. But if you focus on earthly success indicator's and don't understand spiritual significance, you will eventually burn yourself out and come "down on yourself" for not achieving enough.

If you've not always lived your current philosophy, what provoked the change?
I think age does wonders for you. I just turned sixty this year and had a ten-month celebration. In many ways I feel the first fifty-nine years of my life have been preparation for doing the Lord's work. Now the next thirty-five or forty, I think I can really make a contribution. The older I get, the more I believe that if your want to make God laugh, "tell Him your plan." Now I'm ready to live by his plan.

On Og Mandino's
Ten Ancient Scrolls
Ken Blanchard

The real value to anyone reading Og Mandino books is to realize that we're here on earth to serve and help others not to be served. What a different attitude for a sales person. Rather than at the end of the day saying "I wonder what else I can sell today?" to instead say, "I wonder if there is anybody else I can help serve today." Og Mandino's *The Greatest Salesman in the World* was a wonderful perspective setter. We all have been put on earth for a special calling but let's not forget that you can't talk about your calling without talking about the caller, and the caller wants us to serve.

The **3**rd *Scroll* **Persistence**

I will persist until I succeed.

In the Orient young bulls are tested for the fight arena in a certain manner. Each is brought to the ring and allowed to attack a picador who pricks them with a lance. **The bravery of each bull is then rated with care according to the number of times he demonstrates his willingness to charge in spite of the sting of the blade. Henceforth will I recognize that each day I am tested by life in like manner.** If I persist, if I continue to try, if I continue to charge forward, I will succeed.

I will persist until I succeed.

I was not delivered unto this world in defeat, nor does failure course in my veins. **I am not a sheep waiting to be prodded by my shepherd. I am a lion and I refuse to talk, to walk, to sleep with the sheep.** I will hear not those who weep and complain, for their disease is contagious. Let them join the sheep. The slaughterhouse of failure is not my destiny.

I will persist until I succeed.

The prizes of life are at the end of each journey, not near the beginning; and it is not given to me to know how many steps are necessary in order to reach my goal. **Failure I may still encounter at the thousandth step, yet success hides behind the next bend in the road.** Never will I know how close it lies unless I turn the corner.

Always will I take another step. If that is of no avail I will take another, and yet another. In truth, one step at a time is not too difficult.

I will persist until I succeed.

Henceforth, I will consider each day's effort as but one blow of my blade against a mighty oak. The first blow may cause not a tremor in the wood, nor the second, nor the third. **Each blow, of itself, may be trifling, and seem of no consequence. Yet from childish swipes the oak will eventually tumble.** So it will be with my efforts of today.

I will be liken to the raindrop which washes away the mountain; the ant who devours a tiger; the star which brightens the earth; the slave who builds a pyramid. I will build my castle one brick at a time for I know that small attempts, repeated, will complete any undertaking.

I will persist until I succeed.

I will never consider defeat **and I will remove from my vocabulary such words and phrases as quit, cannot, unable, impossible, out of the question, improbable, failure, unworkable, hopeless, and retreat; for they are the words of fools. I will avoid despair but if this disease of the mind should infect me then I will work on in despair.** I will toil and I will endure. I will ignore the obstacles at my feet and keep mine eyes on the goals above my head, for I know that where dry desert ends, green grass grows.

I will persist until I succeed.

I will remember the ancient law of averages and I will bend it to my good. I will persist with knowledge that each failure to sell will increase my chance for success at the next attempt. Each nay I hear will bring me closer to the sound of yea. Each frown I meet only prepares me for the smile to come. Each misfortune I encounter will carry in it the seed of tomorrow's good luck. I must have the night to appreciate the day. I must fail often to succeed only once.

I will persist until I succeed.

I will try, and try, and try again. Each obstacle I will consider as a mere detour to my goal and a challenge to my profession. I will persist and develop my skills as the mariner develops his, by learning to ride out the wrath of each storm.

I will persist until I succeed.

Henceforth, I will learn and apply another secret of those who excel in my work. When each day is ended, not regarding whether it has been a success or a failure, I will attempt to achieve one more sale. When my thoughts beckon my tired body homeward I will resist the temptation to depart. I will try again. I will make one more attempt to close with victory, and if that fails I will make another. Never will I allow any day to end with a failure. Thus will I plant the seed of tomorrow's success and gain an insurmountable advantage over those who cease their labor at a prescribed time. When others cease their struggle, then mine will begin, and my harvest will be full.

I will persist until I succeed.

Nor will I allow yesterday's success to lull me into today's complacency, for this is the great foundation of failure. I will forget the happenings of the day that is gone, whether they were good or bad, and greet the new sun with confidence that this will be the best day of my life.

So long as there is breath in me, that long will I persist. For now I know one of the greatest principles of success; if I persist long enough I will win.

I will persist.

I will win.

Whatever becomes vividly engraved upon your subconscious mind will eventually become a reality in your life!

Persistence
The 3rd Lesson

M any people fail to achieve because they quit before the desired results have been obtained. Every effort we make produces a result, yet seldom do our initial efforts yield the end results we seek.

No great achievement, or great failure, for that matter, has ever been attained without persistence. There are many reasons why people fail to persist. In this chapter we will examine some of their causes and how to avoid them.

The third scroll shows us how to develop persistence and reveals why it is an indispensable quality of a good salesperson. There is a great distinction between being an annoying pest and being tactfully persistent. Sometimes you may find it necessary to become a little of both. The following information will help you sharpen your persistence to a point that can penetrate all forms of sales resistance.

1 The Blade of Rejection

"The bravery of each bull is then rated with care according to the number of times he demonstrates his willingness to charge in spite of the sting of the blade."

Rejection in the sales profession may be likened to sawdust in a lumber mill; it is a natural by-product of the work we do. Persistence is often the only protection you have from the painful effects of rejection, for you can't waste time licking your wounds when you are busy pursuing your prey.

Don't become personally offended if someone declines your offer. Instead, think of some new way to present your offer so that it is more appealing. Or, better yet, find someone else to present it to. Like the bull, develop a thick hide not easily penetrated by the blades of rejection, but be intelligent enough to identify and charge the real target rather than the empty excuses that are sometimes used to divert you.

2 Life Test of Bravery

"Henceforth will I recognize that each day I am tested by life in like manner."

Bravery is only bravery when you are aware that dangers exist, and still you proceed. Every day you are confronted with challenges and each challenge is a test of your bravery. Passing the test promotes you to the next level of achievement and even more difficult challenges. If you fail the test you will simply have to repeat the lesson until you get it right.

Accept the fact that you will be tested and confront the tests bravely; you will eventually pass. Avoiding the tests will not make them go away.

3 | Are You a Lion or a Lamb?

"I am not a sheep waiting to be prodded by my shepherd, I am a lion, and I refuse to talk, to walk, to sleep with the sheep."

Sheep are among the most helpless animals in the world. They require a shepherd for protection, food, and water. A lion, on the other hand, is self-sufficient and is bold enough provide for himself and his family.

To be an effective salesperson you must possess a fierce initiative that allows you to make things happen. Do not possess a sheep's mentality, waiting around until someone else prompts you to act; be the lion and take care of yourself.

4 | Is Failure an Event or Opinion?

"Failure I may still encounter at the thousandth step, yet success hides behind the next bend in the road."

Failure is never failure until it becomes accepted as such. I am often reminded of the persistence of the great inventor Thomas Edison. After thousands of attempts to create the electric light, Mr. Edison didn't consider any of his unsuccessful attempts as failure. In his words, "Every wrong attempt discarded, is another step forward."

Brian Tracy, one of the world's top sales trainers, points out that most sales are made after the fifth attempt to close. However, most salespeople don't attempt to close more than once. Consequently, an embarrassing number of sales are lost simply because the prospect is more prepared with objections than the salesperson is with his responses.

In your search for success, many obstacles will stand between you and your goal. Don't abandon your goals; instead, consider altering the path you are taking to reach them. If you persist, eventually you will find the road to success.

5 | The Blow that Tumbles the Oak

"Each blow, of itself, may be trifling, and seem of nonconsequence. Yet from childish swipes the oak will eventually tumble."

The blow that tumbles the oak tree is not the final blow, but a collective blow. Because of man's impatient human nature, we often have little appreciation for the number of blows that must come in between. Like children, we want what we want right now and become irritated when we don't get it right away.

Instantaneous efforts seldom produce long term benefits; it's the efforts we make over time that usually produce the most permanent results.

Examine the second hand on a watch and note its rapid movement. Although the hour hand moves with the same consistency, because it moves so slowly, you can't see its movement. In this way, every effort you make will produce a result even though it may not be immediately noticeable.

6 | The Vocabulary of Fools

"I will remove from my vocabulary such words and phrases as quit, cannot, unable, impossible, out of the question, improbable, failure, unworkable, hopeless, and retreat, for they are the words of fools."

Every word you speak has a profound effect on two very important areas of your life: the thoughts of the people you speak them to and your own thoughts as well. Your words consistently reflect and affect who you are inside.

One of the quickest ways to alter your view of yourself is to alter the words you speak. Words are thought containers; therefore, words and thoughts have a very interconnected relationship. If you change your thoughts, your words will change, and if you change your words, your thoughts will change.

7 | Working Through Despair
"I will avoid despair but if this disease of the mind should infect me then I will work on in despair."

No matter how hard you try, there is always the possibility that you may occasionally be overtaken by despair. It is like the flu bug, highly contagious and possibly incapacitating. Yet, like the flu, if you build up a strong enough resistance to it, despair will not easily attach itself to you.

Since this is a disease of the mind, you can build up a resistance by filling your mind with positive thoughts. Despair won't survive long in an environment saturated with positive thought impulses.

8 | The Law of Averages
"I will remember the ancient law of averages and I will bend it to my good."

Simply stated, the law of averages is the natural tendency of all sales efforts to yield only a certain percentage of positive results. In order to bend the law of averages in your favor you must first determine your present close ratio. For the sake of this example, let's say you are currently closing one out of five. That would give you a 20 percent close ratio, which means that out of every 100 sales you attempt to make, 20 will actually close.

The important thing is not to be discouraged if every attempt does not produce successful results. In his famous book, *How I Raised*

Myself from Failure to Success in Selling, Frank Bettger points out that every sales attempt he made was worth money to him. Out of 1,849 calls, he conducted 828 interviews. And out of 828 interviews, he closed 65 sales, netting him $4,251.82. Therefore, every call he made generated an average of $2.30 for him regardless of whether or not he received a positive response.

9 | The Secret of Sales Success
"Henceforth, I will learn and apply another secret of those who excel in my work."

The secret that separates a successful salesperson from an ordinary salesperson is that a successful salesperson will always try one more time.

Today's successful salesperson does not walk away from the sale because the prospect has said his first "No." The successful salesperson will try again. And if the sale does not close, he or she will move on to the next prospect, and then try again tomorrow.

10 | The Dark Side of Success
"Nor will I allow yesterday's success to lull me into today's complacency, for this is the great foundation of failure."

The rapid pace of progress does not afford us the luxury of glorying in the achievements of days gone by. Unless you continue to progress, you will lose ground because the world around you will not stand still. Those who waste their time relishing the success of yesterday will soon become have-beens. It is the constant striving toward new achievements that keeps us alive.

The dark side of success comes from the emptiness often experienced after achieving a major goal. Without new aims to reach for there is danger of becoming complacent in what you have already achieved. Truly successful people never stop growing because their dreams are compelling enough to keep them reaching for more. Continue to create new goals and expand your dreams so that you avoid falling into the trap of complacency.

❗ Developing Persistence:
❚ A Practical Exercise

Now, let's look at a practical exercise that can help you increase your powers of persistence. To paraphrase a statement I made earlier, we are all willing to persist if we believe we can win.

Think about it for a moment; the only reason people stop trying is to avoid failure. For instance, if you were on a road sure to lead to the fulfillment of your dreams, would you ever consider getting off that road? Or would you stop and turn around for no apparent reason? Not for a minute! Not unless you thought there was a possibility you wouldn't reach your desired destination.

The mind has an incredible ability to visualize the future; it can see the end result before steps have been taken to get there. A sculptor can look at a jagged stone and see a beautiful statue. It requires a collection of blows over a period of time to produce the result. Likewise, a salesperson can see ultimate success, yet reaching this success requires a collection of reactions over a period of time.

I am going to share with you ten different closing techniques. You probably already have a few techniques of your own. Nevertheless, you should memorize at least six techniques so that you will always be able to make more than five attempts. When you make your attempt to close, don't become discouraged if you don't close the sale. Remember, don't seek the result; seek the reaction. If the reaction you get is not the one you want, simply try another action to produce a different reaction. Every attempt you make will give you a greater control and confidence in the sales process. Thus, you cannot fail; you can only learn.

The following are ten closing techniques.

1. *The assumptive close—Refer to your product as if the prospect already owns it.*
2. *The alternative choice close—Offer at least two options for the prospect.*
3. *The multiple question close—Ask several questions to which the prospect will say yes.*
4. *The sharp angle close—Ask for commitment if you can resolve their objection.*
5. *The direct question close—Ask prospect to purchase your product or service.*
6. *The higher authority close—Show prospect that others they respect have bought.*
7. *The test close—Ask a series of questions to gauge the level of prospect's interest.*
8. *The price close—Show prospect that the price will fit within his allotted budget.*
9. *The take away close—Suggest that the product or offer may no longer be available.*
10. *The Ben Franklin close—List the pros and cons connected to making the purchase.*

Joe Girard

"The World's Greatest Salesman"

J oe Girard had reached a point in his life when he would park his car blocks away and sneak to his own house through the alley in order to keep his car from being repossessed. Then one night he came home and his wife June asked him for money to buy groceries. He didn't have any. "What are the kids going to eat?" she asked. At that moment, all the other problems in his life seemed unimportant. All he could think about was finding some honest way to get food for his family. That was the turning point from which he eventually became the world's greatest salesman. Joe Girard has always believed that smart work and persistence can work wonders, and he has proven this premise with his own life. Starting as shoeshine boy, Joe Girard worked as a newsboy for the *Detroit Free Press* at the age of nine, and then as a dishwasher, delivery boy, stove assembler, and home building contractor before starting a new career as a salesman with a Chevrolet dealership in Eastpointe, Michigan.

Before leaving the dealership he sold 13,001 cars in his fifteen-year career, including 1,425 cars in 1973, a record that put him in the *Guinness Book of World Records* as "The World's Greatest Salesman" for twelve consecutive years. He still holds the all-time record for big-ticket sales, an average of six a day! One of America's most sought-after speakers, Joe Girard appears before civic groups, religious organizations, and sales conventions of many major corporations. His list of engagements include such important companies as Brunswick, General Motors, Sea Ray Boats, Hewlett-Packard, Ford Motor Company, Sears, CBS records, Kraft, Ameritech Publishing (Yellow Pages), Polaroid, Dun & Bradstreet, Kiwanis Club, National Home Builders Association, Chrysler Corporation, Kmart, Mary Kay Cosmetics, General Electric, 3-M, International Racquet & Sports Association, IBM and several hundred advertising and sales clubs worldwide.

It is easy to understand why Joe Girard's first best-selling book, *How To Sell Anything To Anybody,* helped millions of salespeople all over the world, for it is here as well as in his following books, *How To Sell Yourself, How To Close Every Sale, and Mastering Your Way To The Top,* that Mr. Girard reveals the secrets of his success. "People don't buy a product; they buy me, Joe Girard."

Mr. Girard's list of awards is exceptional, including the "Number One" car salesman title every year since 1966, as well as The Golden Plate Award from the American Academy of Achievement. He was nominated for the Horatio Alger Award by the late Dr. Norman Vincent Peale (author of *The Power of Positive Thinking*), and the late Lowell Thomas, the world's first radio broadcaster.

! | Discovering the Secrets
• | of the Successful

How did you get started in the field of sales?
I lost my building business then came home one day and there was no food in the house. I started selling cars so that I could bring home a bag of groceries.

What is the greatest challenge you have had to face over the years?
To prove to my father that I was not a worthless human being.

What do you consider to be the most outstanding achievement of your career?
Receiving the number one sales award and being put into the *Guinness Book of World Records* as the World's number one retail salesperson in the world.

Who were some of your most influential role models and mentors?
My mother and Dr. Norman Vincent Peale, the author of *The Power of Positive Thinking* were my most influential role models.

What is the most effective sales technique you have ever used?
SERVICE, SERVICE, SERVICE!

Give an example of how you would apply this technique in a real life situation? Really love people and go that extra mile for everyone.

What is the most valuable advice you can offer an aspiring sales person? Stay focused and true to yourself. Don't listen to the negative comments of other salespeople and stay away from the stinken-thinken.

If you have not always lived by your current philosophy, what provoked the change?

The thing that changed my life was my mother constantly telling me you can accomplish things and that I would become somebody one day.

_O n   O g   M a n d i n o ' s_
Ten Ancient Scrolls
Joe Girard

No one can achieve lasting success in the field of sales without applying these principles on a regular basis. These are the same principles that I have applied for years. It is because of these principles that I have been able to achieve a level of success which most sales people only dream of.

The 4th Self-Esteem Scroll

I am nature's greatest miracle.

Since the beginning of time never has there been another with my mind, my heart, my eyes, my ears, my hands, my hair, my mouth. **None that came before, none that live today, and none that come tomorrow can walk and talk and move and think exactly like me.** All men are my brothers yet I am different from each. I am a unique creature.

I am nature's greatest miracle.

Although I am of the animal kingdom, animal rewards alone will not satisfy me. Within me burns a flame, which has been passed from generations uncounted, and its heat is a constant irritation to my spirit to become better than I am, and I will. I will fan this flame of dissatisfaction and proclaim my uniqueness to the world.

None can duplicate my brush strokes, none can make my chisel marks, none can duplicate my handwriting, none can produce my child, and, in truth, none has the ability to sell exactly as I. **Henceforth I will**

capitalize on this difference for it is an asset to be promoted to the fullest.

I am nature's greatest miracle.

Vain attempts to imitate others no longer will I make. Instead will I place my uniqueness on display in the market place. I will proclaim it, yea, I will sell it. I will begin now to accent my differences; hide my similarities. So too will I apply this principle to the goods I sell. Salesman and goods, different from all others, and proud of the difference.

I am a unique creature of nature.

I am rare, and there is value in all rarity; therefore, I am valuable. **I am the end product of thousands of years of evolution; therefore, I am better equipped in both mind and body than all the emperors and wise men who preceded me.**

But my skills, my mind, my heart, and my body will stagnate, rot, and die lest I put them to good use. **I have unlimited potential. Only a small portion of my brain do I employ; only a paltry amount of my muscles do I flex.** A hundredfold or more can I increase my accomplishments of yesterday and this I will do, beginning today. Nevermore will I be satisfied with yesterday's accomplishments nor will I indulge, anymore, in self-praise for deeds which in reality are too small to even acknowledge. I can accomplish far more than I have, and I will, for why should the miracle which produced me end with my birth?

Why can I not extend that miracle to my deeds of today?

I am nature's greatest miracle.

I am not on this earth by chance. I am here for a purpose and that purpose is to grow into a mountain, not to shrink to a grain of sand. Henceforth will I apply all my efforts to become the highest mountain of all and I will strain my potential until it cries for mercy. **I will increase my knowledge of mankind, myself, and the goods I sell, thus my sales will multiply. I will practice, and improve, and polish the words I utter to sell my goods, for this is the foundation on which I will build my career** and never will I forget that many have attained great wealth and success with only one sales talk, delivered with excellence. Also will I seek constantly to improve my manners and graces, for they are the sugar to which all are attracted.

I am nature's greatest miracle.

I will concentrate my energy on the challenge of the moment and my actions will help me forget all else. The problems of my home will be left in my home. I will think naught of my family when I am in the market place for this will cloud my thoughts. So too will the problems of the market place be left in the market place and I will think naught of my profession when I am in my home for this will dampen my love.

There is no room in the market place for my family, nor is there room in my home for the market. Each I will divorce from the other and thus will I remain wedded to both. Separate must they remain or my career will die. This is a paradox of the ages.

I am nature's greatest miracle.

I have been given eyes to see and a mind to think and now **I know a great secret of life for I perceive, at last, that all my problems, discouragements, and heartaches are, in truth, great opportunities in disguise.** I will no longer be fooled by the garments they wear for mine eyes are open. I will look beyond the cloth and I will not be deceived.

I am nature's greatest miracle.

No beast, no plant, no wind, no rain, no rock, no lake had the same beginning as I, for **I was conceived in love and brought forth with a purpose.** In the past I have not considered this fact but it will henceforth shape and guide my life.

I am nature's greatest miracle.

And nature knows not defeat. Eventually, she emerges victorious and so will I, and with each victory the next struggle becomes less difficult.

I will win, and I will become a great salesman, for I am unique.

I am nature's greatest miracle.

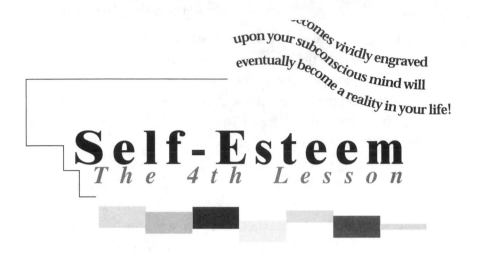

Self-Esteem
The 4th Lesson

What we achieve or fail to achieve in life does not depend upon who we are; it depends on who "**we think**" we are. The view we have of ourselves inwardly is what determines the personal qualities and characteristics we display outwardly. The **self** we display openly before the world is what determines how the world responds to us.

Merely analyzing our strengths and weaknesses does not give us an accurate picture of who we really are. *In The Greatest Miracle in the World,* Og Mandino proclaims the profound truth, "You are more than a human being, you are a human becoming."

The fourth scroll presents a clearer picture of your unlimited and untapped potential. By giving you a better idea of what you have the potential to become, this scroll will elevate your self-esteem and enhance your ability to unleash your true potential. Once you know what you have the ability to become, you will never be the same.

1 | Your Un-Duplicatable Uniqueness

"None that came before, none that live today, and none that come tomorrow can walk and talk and move and think exactly like me."

Consider your uniqueness a tremendous value. Not doing so is like ignoring a one-of-a-kind, priceless work of art. Without awareness of your personal value, you will sell yourself for much less than you are worth. When you begin to think highly of yourself, others will value you highly as well.

2 | Exploiting Your Diversity

"Henceforth, I will capitalize on this difference for it is an asset to be promoted to the fullest."

We strive to be like everyone else, to fit in with the crowd, to be accepted. Yet, when we find ourselves trying to be like others, it's a sure sign that we haven't accepted ourselves for who we are.

Highlight your differences; they are what set you apart. Examine your product or service and identify the distinguishing features that separate it from the others. This is your unique selling point. Uniqueness alone can be a sufficient reason for people to buy from you. Is your product newer, older, larger, smaller, less expensive or more extravagant? Regardless of what the difference may be, you have something that no one else on earth has, and if you can exploit it effectively, the world will reward you handsomely for it.

3 | Your Level of Evolutionary Growth

"I am the end product of thousands of years of evolution; therefore, I am better equipped in both mind and body than all the emperors and wise men who preceded me."

Today's youth are exposed to more information daily than our great grandparents may have been exposed to in a lifetime. Because we live in an era marked by such amazing technological advancements, we are at a greater advantage than preceding generations. Sometimes such advantages can make people apathetic. Instead of striving to continue this process of growth, they simply rest upon the achievements of others.

It is your responsibility to continue the development of humanity's evolutionary growth so that future generations may benefit from the progress you make during the course of your existence.

4 | Your Untapped Potential

"I have unlimited potential. Only a small portion of my brain do I employ; only a paltry amount of my muscles do I flex."

Scientists have discovered that throughout a lifetime the average person will use less than ten percent of his brain capacity. Your challenge is to discover new ways to unlock this unlimited potential. Such a tremendous challenge will do wonders for your self-esteem. When you are preoccupied with searching out the limits of your untapped potential you will discover capabilities that you may have never imagined you possessed.

Right now there is unlimited potential within you, the ability to solve problems that you have not yet encountered. Look for new ways to exercise this potential by finding problems to resolve and by so doing you will greatly increase your own capacity to perform.

5 | The Power of Product Knowledge

"I will increase my knowledge of mankind, myself, and the goods I sell, thus my sales will multiply."

Developing sufficient product knowledge is one of the most important steps in mastering the sales process. Knowing your product or service enables you to have greater confidence in making the sales presentation. Your confidence and ability to answer prospects' questions effectively will help them to trust you and rely on your insight as an expert in your field. Once you have established a level of trust with your prospects, they will be more receptive to any comments or suggestions you make.

A general knowledge of human nature will go a long way in helping you deal with any prospect, and having knowledge of their specific needs is just as important as product knowledge. However, you must be careful not to treat every prospect the same; recognize and appreciate their unique differences.

6 | Mastering Your Craft

"I will practice, and improve, and polish the words I utter to sell my goods, for this is the foundation on which I will build my career."

Mastery is unattainable without intensive practice. Even geniuses, blessed with natural talent, must practice to become masters in their field. Words are to the salesperson what an instrument is to the musician, and unless you develop the ability to use them skillfully, you can never hope to make much more than noise.

In order to master the sales process you must learn to master the sales presentation. The sales presentation is much more that just telling someone about your product or service. All sales masters agree that telling is not selling. Selling requires you to ask carefully designed questions with the same precision that a skilled lawyer might use in questioning a witness. You must know the answers before you ask the questions, and you must be able to anticipate your prospect's responses. The only way you can develop this degree of mastery is by practicing your presentation over and over again.

7 | The Paradox of the Ages

"There is no room in the market place for my family, nor is there room in my home for the market. Each I will divorce from the other and thus will I remain wedded to both."

Though your family and career are equally important, there is often great danger when they begin to overlap. One danger lies in confusion caused when you are forced to choose one over the other.

Since both of these elements are so vitally important in your life, the temptation to value one over the other can often cause a short circuit in your thinking. The secret to managing both of these effectively is to devote separate quality time and attention to each.

8 | The Opportunity in all Opposition

"I know a great secret of life for I perceive, at last, that all my problems, discouragements, and heartaches are, in truth, great opportunities in disguise."

We all have a natural tendency to avoid opposition because it is easier to travel the path of least resistance. You could say that opposition is the fertilizer of growth, for though it may not be very appealing, it actually causes us to expand our abilities.

In the words of Napoleon Hill, "In every opposition there exists the seed of an equivalent benefit." The trick is to look at the opposition in a way that will enable you to uncover the benefit it contains.

9 | The By-Product of Love
"I was conceived in love and brought forth with a purpose."

In his book, *The Greatest Miracle in the World,* Og Mandino describes the act of conception with these words: "From your father in his moment of supreme love, flowed countless seeds of love, more than four hundred million in number. All of them, as they swam within your mother, gave up the ghost and died. All except one. You!"

There is no question that the creation of a life is one of the most miraculous things known to mankind. What's even more amazing is that it occurs as a result of the ultimate expression of love between two people. Such an encounter could not possibly produce an outcome that is less than phenomenal. Regardless of the circumstances surrounding your birth, the fact that you are here is evidence that your life is the result of a miracle.

If your very existence is the consequence of a miracle then you yourself must also be miraculous. Just the thought of how you came into being should be strong motivation to encourage you to reach for your greatest potential.

10 | The Undefeatable Quality of Nature
"I am nature's greatest miracle. And nature knows not defeat. Eventually she emerges victorious and so will I."

You are an intriguing part of a natural phenomenon. Just as the awesome forces of nature cannot be completely harnessed, the forces that stir within you cannot be subdued by the circumstances surrounding you. All of creation demonstrates the relentless power of nature, and since you are a part of creation, this same power resides within you and should be demonstrated by you as well.

No matter how many natural disasters scar the face of the earth,

Mother Nature continues to use the seasons to heal her wounds. Likewise, regardless of the many defeats and setbacks you may encounter along the path to success, be assured that your victory is also inevitable.

❗•| Developing Self-Esteem
| A Practical Exercise

The number one cause of low self-esteem is the tendency to estimate our value by taking an inventory of the things we do not possess. Too often we compare ourselves with other people and only notice those areas where we seem to fall short. We may see ourselves as not being as healthy, wealthy, or as wise as someone else.

If you think this way, you will only highlight your deficiencies and ultimately lower your self-esteem. Instead, take an inventory of what you do possess – not just material possessions, but what you have in every area of your life that makes you rich.

Take a moment to inventory your assets.
1. List ten things that you are proud to have achieved.
2. List five of your most positive and virtuous characteristics.
3. List three important goals that you set and accomplished within the last year.
4. Name seven of your most valued personal acquaintances.
5. List two of the most important lessons you have ever learned.
6. What is the most valuable idea you had in the last year?
7. Name one major tragedy or setback that you have been able to survive.
8. What is the most important contribution you have made to your community?
9. What are three areas you have shown the most improvement in over the last year?

10. If you died today what would have been your greatest contribution to humanity?

Reviewing this list will lift your self-esteem when it is low, and updating your personal inventory will make your self-esteem grow. Once a month, take time out to review your progress of the previous month and make plans for the coming month. During this time go over your self-inventory again. Regularly performing this exercise will motivate you to do positive things so that you will have them to record.

To build your confidence and self-esteem in your professional activity, you need to become expert in your field. The following are steps you can take to achieve that goal.

1. Identify and memorize three key features about your product or service.
2. Identify and memorize three benefits of your product or service.
3. Identify three of the most frequent objections to your product or service.
4. Memorize three patented responses to those objections.
5. Collect three or more unique facts about your product or service.
6. Create a list of ten frequently asked questions and know the answers.
7. Collect quotations from noted authorities in your field.
8. Join an industry trade association and subscribe to a trade publication.
9. Read some of the leading books on your professional subject.
10. Attend seminars and lectures that deal with your industry.

Mark Victor Hansen

Author • Speaker • Sales Trainer • Entrepreneur

*M*ark Victor Hansen's new business hit $2 million in sales within three years. Then in 1974 the Arab oil embargo suddenly caused a key product he needed for his business to be in scarce supply. Overnight Hansen was out of business and both he and his company fell into bankruptcy. He lost his car, some of his clothes and needed to borrow money just to eat. He lived in the hallway of his friend's apartment for six months. Then one day Hansen heard a tape by Cavett Robert, a motivational speaker, and he listened to it more than 280 times. Being inspired by the message, Hansen picked himself up out of the stairwell and followed Cavett into the speaking business. The rest, as they say, is motivational history. Many people go through life and never experience their true calling. Mark Victor Hansen is a man who is one of the few to find his absolute life's work. For more than 20 years, Mark has focused on the vital elements of human behavior that most effect the outcome of a personal and professional life.

Mark Victor Hansen is in high demand as a keynote speaker and seminar leader by many of North America's top corporations and professional associations. He is known as The Master Motivator, and for good reason. During his career of over two decades, his message has

reached over 1 million people, live, worldwide and virtually every major city in the United States and Canada. Over 150 audiences a year are stimulated to personal and professional success by his electrifying presentation style, sprinkled with humor, and loaded with empowerment strategies, and thought provoking substance.

He has also made a profound difference through his empowering library of learning materials. These programs are often utilized as a key component in corporate sales training. In addition to his recorded materials, Mark is also a prolific writer with many best-selling books. Since it's publication date in June 1993, *Chicken Soup for the Soul, 101 Stories to Open the Heart and Rekindle the Spirit,* has sold over 6 million copies and continues to top the best-seller lists nationwide. With universal themes from love and positive attitude to humor and relationships - these stories touch people from all walks of life. *Chicken Soup for the Soul* has been awarded "1994 Book of the Year" by over 20,000 bookstores nationwide. It's sequel, *A Second Helping of Chicken Soup* is a runaway best seller as well. Debuting on the same national lists, it has sold over 2 million copies since April 1995. Additional books by Mark are *The Aladdin Factor, The Master Motivator, and Chicken Soup for the Soul Cookbook.* Mark has been a member of the National Speakers Association since 1974, having earned a C.S.P. (Certified Speaking Professional) which has been achieved by less than seven percent of their membership.

! | Discovering the Secrets
• | of the Successful

How did you get started in the field of sales?

I have been selling since I was nine years old. When I was in Europe I saw these low handle bar racing bicycles and I asked my father for one. He said "you can have it when you're 21 or you can have one now if you earn it yourself." I found out that you could sell greeting cards on consignment. I looked in the dictionary and found out that the word consignment meant that they would give you the cards, you sell them and then send in the money, so I though "hey I can afford this" and I did it. I went door to door doing my little presentation and basically no one would say no to me. We were only supposed to sell in our own neighborhoods, but I got so involved in it that I went all over. People invited me into their houses, listened to my story and though I was an industrious little fellow so they bought my cards. To make a long story short I become the number one greeting card sales person at nine and I thought to myself "hey this is pretty cool, I could do this for rest of my life." Little did I know that that is what I would spend the rest of my life doing. Since that humble beginning we have sold over 50 million Chicken Soup books, so I think we have done pretty well.

What is the greatest challenge that you have had to face over the years?

I would say that my greatest challenge is the fact that I have more opportunity than any other man that walks on the planet right now. As a result, I have to often say no to stuff that I want to say yes to. Things that I like and believe in but because I am so deep into my own stuff but I just don't have the time. For instance we have 74 new Chicken Soup titles that we are working on. I have also gone back to making tapes, and I will give you three of the up coming titles: *How to Think Bigger Than You Ever Thought You Could Think, How to Up Your Self Worth, Net Worth and Life Worth,* and then there is *Your First Million, 12 Ways to Make a Million.*

What do you consider to be your most outstanding achievement of your career?

Talking to you right now. The fact that anyone would find me interesting enough to want to interview and talk to me is beyond me. I think every interview is a cherished event and I feel that I am in the right place at this exact moment in the universe.

Who were some of your most influential role models and mentors?

When I was in graduate school getting my doctorate Dr. R Buckminster Fuller was it, to me he could walk on water. As a writer I consider Og Mandino as one of the greatest of all time. My writing partner Jack Canfield is a total mentor and mensch. Mensch is a Jewish term meaning you have got it together, your someone who is totally likable and has really good resources. As a speaker the guy that launched me was Cavett Robert.

Cavett was a founder of the National Speakers Association and he taught guys like Zig Ziglar and myself how to sell from the platform, he created an industry which didn't exist thirty years ago but which today is doing over a hundred and ten billion dollars a year.

What is the most effective sales technique you have ever used?

Ask for the order. We wrote a book called the *Aladdin Factor* and it teaches all the ways to ask. In fact Nightingale Conant just signed a contract with us to put the book into a six tape set because they thought it was so good. The fact of the matter is everyone is taught not to ask, for instance as a child we are taught not to talk to strangers, but if you're going to be in sales everyone is going to be a stranger. The spiritual phrase is ask and you shall receive, most people ask once and then stop. You've just got to keep asking and then ask better than you have asked before and have fun asking.

Give an example of how you would apply this technique in a real life situation?

When I started in the speaking business twenty-five years ago, I had no money, I didn't have a brochure, I had a beat up car and one suit with holes in the pants pockets and everywhere else. I was under charging my customers. I would go to the owner of a small insurance company and say, "Sir do you want more sales out of your sales people?" Needless to say their response would be "Yes." I'd reply "Then there are four basic areas we need to talk about, prospecting, presenting, persuading or actually closing and good work habits, which one do you think your people need most?" I would schedule the meeting and then say, "by the way your investment is only twenty-five dollars a seminar." Since then things have gotten better and now I charge twenty thousand dollars an hour.

What is the most valuable advice you can offer an aspiring sales person?

The most important thing you can do is be a good mentee then a great mentor. Be a good student to a great sales person that is selling whatever it is you desire to sell. Carry their suitcase or do whatever you have to do but watch and pick up on their work style and life style. Be a good apprentice, ask all the questions and work as closely as you can with them so you can learn how they do what they do.

If you have not always lived by your current philosophy, what provoked the change?

Two things, one is seminars. I think everybody needs to go to a seminar at least once a month because leaders are born at seminars, like the kind I did last night. A good seminar winds people up and sends them out saying and believing they can walk on water and even fly. Number two is you have got to listen to audio tapes everyday for a least an hour. All of us drive about two hours a day. You should make that seven hundred hours a year that you spend in your car a classroom on wheels. Listen to people who have done what you want to do and you will do well. Because of audio tape learning I have made a fortune in five different markets, a fortune in speaking, in writing, in real-estate, in network marketing, and in the internet.

Ten Ancient Scrolls

Mark Victor Hansen

O g's ten scrolls are timeless, classic wisdom that are easy and enjoyable to assimilate and use. I love them. In my companies, it is voluntarily mandatory that my teammates read, own and utilize these brilliantly written principles. If everyone conquered the wisdom contained in *The Greatest Salesman in the World*, the world would work at 100 percent. I loved Og and all his works.

The *5*th *Scroll* Time

I will live this day as if it is my last.

And what shall I do with this last precious day, which remains, in my keeping? **First, I will seal up its container of life so that not one drop spills itself upon the sand.** I will waste not a moment mourning yesterday's misfortunes, yesterday's defeats, yesterday's aches of the heart, for **why should I throw good after bad?**

Can sand flow upward in the hourglass? Will the sun rise where it sets and set where it rises? Can I relive the errors of yesterday and right them? Can I call back yesterday's wounds and make them whole? Can I become younger than yesterday? Can I take back the evil that was spoken, the blows that were struck, the pain that was caused? No. Yesterday is buried forever and I will think of it no more.

I will live this day as if it is my last.

And what then shall I do? Forgetting yesterday neither will I think of tomorrow. **Why should I throw now after maybe? Can tomorrow's sand flow through the glass before today's? Will the** sun rise twice this morning? **Can I perform tomorrow's deeds while standing in today's path? Can I place tomorrow's gold in today's purse? Can tomorrow's child be born today? Can tomorrow's death cast its shadow backward and darken today's joy? Should I concern myself over events which I may never witness? Should I torment myself with problems that may never come to pass? No! Tomorrow lies buried with yesterday, and I will think of it no more.**

I will live this day as if it is my last.

This day is all I have and these hours are now my eternity. I greet this sunrise with cries of joy as a prisoner who is reprieved from death. **I lift mine arms with thanks for this priceless gift of a new day.** So too, I will beat upon my heart with gratitude as I consider all who greeted yesterday's sunrise who are no longer with the living today. I am indeed a fortunate man and today's hours are but a bonus, undeserved. **Why have I been allowed to live this extra day when others, far better than I, have departed? Is it that they have accomplished their purpose while mine is yet to be achieved?** Is this another opportunity for me to become the man I know I can be? Is there a purpose in nature? Is this my day to excel?

I will live this day as if it is my last.

I have but one life and life is naught but a measurement of time. When I waste one I destroy the other. If I waste today I destroy the last page of my life. Therefore, each hour of this day will I cherish for it can never return. It cannot be banked today to be withdrawn on the morrow, for who can trap the wind? Each minute of this day will I grasp with both hands and fondle with love for its value is beyond price. What dying man can purchase another breath though he willingly gives all his gold? What price dare I place on the hours ahead? I will make them priceless!

I will live this day as if it is my last.

I will avoid with fury the killers of time. Procrastination I will destroy with action; doubt I will bury under faith; fear I will dismember with confidence. Where there are idle mouths I will listen not; where there are idle hands I will linger not; where there are idle bodies I will visit not. Henceforth I know that to court idleness is to steal food, clothing, and warmth from those I love. I am not a thief. **I am a man of love and today is my last chance to prove my love and my greatness.**

I will live this day as if it is my last.

The duties of today I shall fulfill today. Today I shall fondle my children while they are young; tomorrow they will be gone, and so will I. Today I shall embrace my woman with sweet kisses; tomorrow she will be gone, and so will I. Today I shall lift up a friend in need; tomorrow he will no longer cry for help, nor will I hear his cries. Today I shall give myself in sacrifice and work; tomorrow I will have nothing to give, and there will be none to receive.

I will live this day as if it is my last.

And if it is my last, it will be my greatest monument. This day I will make the best day of my life. This day I will drink every minute to its full. I will savor its taste and give thanks. I will make every hour count and each minute I will trade only for something of value. I will labor harder than ever before and push my muscles until they cry for relief, and then I will continue. **I will make more calls than ever before. I will sell more goods than ever before. I will earn more gold than ever before. Each minute of today will be more fruitful than hours of yesterday.** My last must be my best.

I will live this day as if it is my last.

And if it is not, I shall fall to my knees and give thanks.

Time Management

The 5th Lesson

Whatever becomes vividly engraved upon your subconscious mind will eventually become a reality in your life!

*T*here are many books and lectures on time management. They teach us how to organize our tasks to achieve maximum efficiency and how to juggle our affairs to save as much time as we can. However, most of this information deals with time from an external point of view. The fifth scroll not only gives us time management techniques; it also shows us how to deal with time from an internal point of view. It teaches us how to develop the proper attitude toward time so that we can enjoy every moment to the fullest.

Time itself is not something that can be managed. What we really must learn to do is manage ourselves in the context of time. Time is like a flowing river and we are like ships sailing upon that river. We don't manage the flow of the river; what we manage is the direction of our sail and rudder to determine our destination.

The fifth scroll helps us to put the past, present and future in perspective by teaching us how to manage our attitudes about time. The following points will guide you through this mind management process.

1 | Living in a Day Tight Compartment

"First, I will seal up its container of life so not one drop spills itself upon the sand."

Anxiety is a sickness that cripples daily productivity. Regrets of the past and worries about the future have a way of sapping your energy and limiting the things you can accomplish in the present. Og Mandino often spoke of a practice he developed of living each day in a day tight compartment. This simple method helped him to eliminate the counterproductive side effects caused by anxiety.

Og discovered this principle in an address that Sir William Osler made to the students of Yale University. One day, while on a cruise ship, Sir William observed how the lower compartments are sealed off to keep the ship from sinking if the hull is breached. By closing off the compartments, water can only enter if there is a hole in the ship.

Og used this example to illustrate how we can keep our lives from sinking. By closing off the regrets of the past and worries about the future we can keep our dreams afloat. This attitude enables us to obtain maximum productivity from each day and, as a result, live much more fulfilled lives.

2 | Perspective on Yesterday

"Why should I throw good after bad?...Yesterday is buried forever and I will think of it no more."

A rear view mirror is an important tool in the driving process. It enables the driver to glance at where he has been occasionally without having to take his eyes off where he is going. However, it would be foolish to use your rear view mirror to guide you toward your desired destination. If you were to focus your attention on your rear view mirror, and only occasionally look ahead through the windshield, you would probably have an accident before you made it out of the driveway.

Likewise, the past is an important tool, but if you focus too much attention on it, it will be difficult to guide your life toward your desired destination. If your thoughts are focused on the past, then all of your tomorrows will never look any different than your yesterdays.

3 | Perspective on Tomorrow
"Why should I throw now after maybe?...Tomorrow lies buried with yesterday, and I will think of it no more."

Another destroyer of present productivity is fear of the future. Fear has the same paralyzing effect as regret; every second we waste on fear and regret is a second we could have invested in producing a more fulfilling life.

Most of the things we waste time worrying about never occur, just as many of the things we worry about are things we can't change.

Since it takes no more effort to hope than it does to worry, wouldn't it make sense to use our creative vision to picture the outcomes we desire instead of the ones we fear? Instead of saying, "I will take that positive step that can bring me closer to my goal," say, "I am taking that step today." Then DO IT.

4 | Treasuring the Present
"I lift my arms with thanks for this priceless gift of a new day."

Christmas is one of the most celebrated holidays in the world. It is a day for giving and receiving. Imagine a Christmas of only worn out presents from Christmases past, and a long list of presents you desire for Christmases in the future. Though Christmas is about much more than material gifts, the excitement of the season lies in the presents of the PRESENT, not those of the past and future.

Each day of your life is like a brand new gift. You should not miss out on the enjoyment of unwrapping this present by wasting time pondering over the past and future.

Greet each dawn with the same positive attitude as conveyed in the ancient Indian salutation, "Look to this day, for tomorrow is only a vision and yesterday is already a dream. But if we look well to this day, we can make every tomorrow a vision of hope, and every yesterday a dream of happiness."

5 | Fulfilling your Purpose

"Why have I been allowed to live this extra day when others, far better than I, have departed? Is it that they have accomplished their purpose while mine is yet to be achieved?"

There comes a time in every life when one must search out his or her life's purpose. Once you become clear about your purpose then you must strive daily to invest time and energy toward its fulfillment. You cannot afford to spend an entire day without doing something directly related to accomplishing your purpose. Your purpose will not somehow miraculously fulfill itself, and every day you neglect to work toward it represents a day longer that it will take you to reach your desired destination.

To know your true purpose, you need only to take some quiet time for introspection. Get to know yourself. Your purpose will be obvious, and the more you pursue it, the clearer it will become.

6 | Battling Time Killers

"I will avoid with fury the killers of time. Procrastination I will destroy with action; doubt I will bury under faith; fear I will dismember with confidence."

Notice the direct opposites Og cites as counteractive forces to time killers. To apply these solutions effectively you must first recognize that the problem is not a part of who you are. Too often people see negative qualities as a part of their personality. They say to themselves, "I am a procrastinator, I am doubtful, I am afraid." When you view these qualities as a part of yourself, it becomes difficult to change.

However, when you recognize these negatives as external forces, you can easily counteract them. Procrastination, doubt and fear are like mosquitoes that come and land ever so gently upon you. If you don't shoo them away they will sting you. The counteractive force of action, faith and confidence are like an insecticide with power to kill the pests seeking to kill your time.

Take a close look at your average workday and you can spot the killers that are destroying one of your most precious resources, time. Perhaps it's attending unnecessary meetings, too much unproductive phone time, or just a lack of proper organization. Whatever it is, once you spot it, develop a strategy to combat it. You will add priceless moments to your life.

7 | My Final Opportunity

"I am a man of love and today is my last chance to prove my love and my greatness."

With all the uncertainties in life, people are constantly seeking security, and life's most certain yet most disregarded guarantee is this: One day, life as we know it, will end.

Occasionally you will be forced to come to grips with this reality.

When you are startled by some tragic headline news, when a loved one passes away, or when you have a personal brush with death, you give more consideration to the temporary nature of life. On these occasions you may handle your time more carefully. The thought of life ending somehow motivates you to make the most of each moment.

Now, if this attitude can provoke you to maximize your productivity and obtain greater fulfillment, wouldn't it be wise to maintain this attitude throughout each day of your life? I don't suggest that you become obsessed with death, but rather let your awareness of the inevitability of death inspire you to live every day as if it were your final opportunity, because it could very well be.

8 | Managing Yourself in Time
"The duties of today I shall fulfill today."

One of the greatest time stealers of all is neglecting to identify the duties we need to perform each day. To awaken each day with no clear-cut plan of action is to invite aimlessness, which is always accompanied by emptiness and confusion.

The simple act of identifying your specific tasks is like placing your hands firmly on the steering wheel of a moving car. By guiding yourself in the direction you wish to travel today, you will be setting a course toward success for tomorrow.

Act on your freedom to identify and execute the duties that must be performed in order to reach your goals in all areas of your life. Don't get caught up in spending years of your life without taking a close look at where your actions are taking you.

9 | The Best Day of Your Life
"And if it is my last it will be my greatest monument. This day I will make the best day of my life."

Here is one verse of a poem I once wrote about time that goes like this:

When you're someplace you don't want to be, it seems like an eternity, yet there is never enough time to do all the things which interest you. How much we have I do not know and when I'd like to take it slow, I wonder, is time on my side?

Time is a devouring beast, for it has caused my now to cease, he swallowed it up in yesterday, that's how my time has gotten away. Yet as I stand here presently, waiting to see the future be, I wonder, is time on my side?

History has been used to teach, and show us how we now can reach, the goals, which in the past we missed, and regret as we reminisce. But in spite of every past mistake, life still goes on and new days break, and perhaps I'll do much better this time.

For all I really have is now, and what I do determines how the mark will look I leave behind, and what will result from my time. So I will take my now to bend and shape, and make what some mistake for fate, now while I still have time!

A conscious attempt to make each day better than the previous one creates a standard of progress which drives us toward daily improvement. Such a habit can enable you to awaken each day with strong anticipation that it will indeed be the best day of your life.

10 | The Appreciated Value of Today
"I will make more calls than ever before, I will sell more goods than ever before, I will earn more gold than ever before. Each minute of today will be more fruitful than the hours of yesterday."

Many years ago one of my mentors gave me some profound insight on how I could increase my value in every area of my life. "You only have to do one thing," he said. Eager to discover this mysterious secret that could dramatically improve my life, I replied "What is this one thing?"

At the time his answer seemed ridiculous, yet over the years I have found his advice to be priceless. His answer was simple, *"Just do one extra thing each day that you did not do yesterday."*

Growth is a universal pattern. If you truly desire success, you must follow the pattern of growth reflected in all nature. And if you make a conscious effort to improve your performance each day, you are guaranteed to appreciate in value as the days go by. By learning to appreciate the value of time, it will become your faithful friend, gracefully carrying you to the shores of the success you desire.

! | Developing Time:
• | A Practical Exercise

In sales, as in any profession, there are a series of tasks that you need to perform on a regular basis. Depending upon the type of product or service you are selling, these tasks may need to be repeated on a weekly or even daily basis. By developing the habit of performing these tasks with the necessary frequency, you eliminate the need to write them on your "to do" list.

The tasks we identify for this particular exercise must be tasks directly related to making sales. Perhaps you spend a certain amount of time making phone calls, sending e-mail and faxes, or mailing correspondences. Maybe you spend time in the field making cold calls, servicing clients or delivering presentations. Create a schedule for these activities, identifying a specific time of day and a specific length of time in which you will address them.

Write your schedule out but make it comfortable for you. If you need to revise it a few times before you get it right, do so. Once you have designed a schedule that works well for you, continue to follow it until you can keep on schedule without referring to your written notes. Soon the schedule will become a habit, and it will keep you productively engaged in your work, even when you're not consciously aware of it.

In his book, *Selling for Dummies,* Tom Hopkins reveals seven standard components of every selling cycle. I have paraphrased them for this exercise. All steps should be part of a salesperson's schedule.

1) Prospect

Identify and locate the potential buyers for your products or services.

2) Make Contact

Make a good first impression on your prospective customer.

3) Qualify Prospect

Make sure you're talking to the right person and assess his or her need for your goods.

4) Presentation

Address the prospect's needs and reveal how your goods can effectively meet them.

5) Address Concerns

Respond to the questions or objections that may follow your presentation.

6) The Close

Complete the steps required to finalize the sale.

7) Referrals

Ask for names of others who might need your product or service.

Though the steps you take in the sales process may differ slightly, the key is to identify the tasks required to make sales and perform them repeatedly until they become habitual.

S p o t l i g h t   o n :

Tom Hopkins
The World's Leading Sales Trainer

T om Hopkins is the epitome of success. A millionaire by the time he reached the age of 27, Hopkins is president of his own company, Tom Hopkins International. Thirty-three years ago, Tom Hopkins considered himself a failure. He had dropped out of college after 90 days and for the next 18 months carried steel on construction sites to make a living.

Believing there had to be a better way to earn a living, he went into sales -- and ran into the worst period of his life. For six months, Hopkins earned an average of $42 a month and slid deeper into debt and despair. Pulling together his last few dollars, he invested in a five-day sales training seminar that turned his life around. In the next six months, Hopkins sold more than $1 million worth of $25,000 homes.

At age 21, he won the Los Angeles Sales and Marketing Institute's coveted SAMMY Award and began setting records in sales performance that still stand today. Because of his unique ability to share his enthusiasm for the profession of selling and the successful selling techniques he developed, Hopkins began giving seminars in 1974. Training as many as 10,000 salespersons a month, he quickly became known as

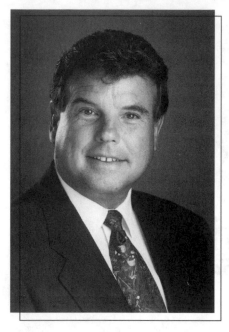

the world's leading sales trainer. Today, as chairman of Tom Hopkins International, he presents approximately 75 seminars a year throughout the United States, Canada, Australia, New Zealand, Singapore and Malaysia.

Hopkins was a pioneer in producing high quality audio and videotape programs for those who could not attend his seminars or who wanted reinforcement after a seminar. Recognized as the most effective sales training programs ever produced, they are continually updated and are now being utilized by over a million people worldwide.

Hopkins also has authored seven books, including *How To Master The Art Of Selling*™ published in 1980. Most recently, Tom authored, *Selling for Dummies*™ for IDG Books Worldwide.

! • | Discovering the Secrets of the Successful

How did you get started in the field of sales?

My dad had been in sales and I didn't need any specific education or experience to get started.

What is the greatest challenge you have had to face over the years?

Maintaining balance between my business and personal life.

What do you consider to be the most outstanding achievement of your career?

I have been blessed to have reached many people with my message and shown them how to build better lives for themselves and their families.

Who were some of you most influential role models and mentors?

J. Douglas Edwards, Earl Nightingale and Zig Ziglar.

What is the most effective sales technique you have used?

The old Ben Franklin balance sheet. Many people hesitate on making decisions because they don't see the answer clearly. This strategy simplifies the benefits.

Give an example of how you would apply this technique in a real life situation?

Here's an example of how to use the Benjamin Franklin technique. This story with Kevin and Karen Smith in a real estate office appeared in my book *SELLING FOR DUMMIES*™.

> **Tom:** Do you think that the home on Third Street might be the best decision for your family?
>
> **Kevin:** Well, Tom, you know that home is a pretty big invest-ment. I don't know that I'm ready to make a decision on this right now. *I've asked a lot of questions up to this point, and*

now I'm ready to put the answers to work for me to close the sale. I can see that he and Karen really don't want make the final decision. They're impressed with the home. They need to get the family moved quickly. The numbers work out. But they're trying to avoid committing to the home. In other words, they are behaving like typical buyers. This is a perfect opportunity for the Benjamin Franklin decision-making process.

Tom: Could it possibly be, Karen and Kevin, that the problem is that you haven't had a chance to weigh the facts involved?

Kevin: Yeah, I don't think we've really gotten to the heart of this thing yet.

Tom: Well, a decision is only as good as the facts on which it's based.

Karen: I think that's probably true.

Tom: You know, it's interesting. Awhile back I was reminded of a man we Americans have long considered one of our wisest men Benjamin Franklin. What Ben used to do when he was uncertain about making a decision was to take a sheet of paper and draw a line right down the middle. On one side of the page he would write all the reasons in favor of the decision. While on the other he would write all the reasons against the decision. Then he would simply add up the reasons on each side, and see which decision was the best.

It's a funny thing. One day I decided to try Ben's system, not only in my professional life but in my personal life, as well. Pretty soon, my whole family was using it to make all kinds of decisions. Would it be okay with you if we tried it now just to get a feel for the facts of your decision? Ben Franklin said that if a decision was the right thing to do, he wanted to be sure to go ahead with it. If it was wrong, he wanted to be sure to avoid it. So why don't we analyze the decision and "get down to the heart of it." As you put it?

Kevin and Karen: Okay, yeah, let's do that

Tom: Great. So the reasons for the decision go on one side, and all those against the decision go on the other side. Then you can add up the columns and the right decision should be clear. We have time, don't we? It'll take us just a couple of minutes.

Kevin: Yeah okay. *I have a long list of things they like about the home because I've made notes on every positive comment they've made since we drove into the neighborhood. If they run out of positives off the tops of their heads, I'll remind them of those on my list.*

Tom: Okay, let's start it off here. Let's think of the reasons favoring the decision. You agree that the home has all the features you were looking for, isn't that right?

Karen: Yes, it does.

Tom: And we've already established that with the right financing you could actually have a smaller monthly investment than what you have on the home you're in now.

Kevin and Karen: Right.

Tom: You said you wanted to be close to the elementary school and this home is just three blocks away. That's certainly a plus, don't you think?

Kevin and Karen: Absolutely.

Tom: Let's go on. You thought the professional landscaping in the backyard was impressive.

Karen: Yeah, the kids would have a lot of fun in that yard,

Tom: Wouldn't they? Let's write that down. And what about the outside of the home? When we first pulled up, Karen, remember how you got so excited?

Karen: It really is a beautiful home.

Tom: Let's see; that's five. Can you think of any others?

Kevin: Well, we really liked the extras in the newly remodeled kitchen.

Tom: All right. We'll put that down.

Kevin: I like all the big trees on the property.

Tom: Okay. We'll put that down, too.

Karen: Oh! We both liked the sunken bathtub in the master bathroom.

Tom: Great. Is there anything else you can think of? Now, how many reasons can you come up with on the negative side?

Kevin: Well, let's see. The down payment is a concern. It's almost all we've saved.

Tom: Okay, what else?

Kevin: We were really interested in finding a home that had solar heating.

Tom: Those are both valid points, Kevin. Can you come up with any others? *After a pause, it's obvious that Karen and Kevin aren't coming up with any more concerns.*

Tom: All right. Why don't we just add these up? Karen, Kevin, don't you think the answer is rather obvious?

What is the most valuable advice you can offer an aspiring sales person?

Unlike when I started out, today there are many great books, tapes, and trainers to learn from. Don't go by trial and error.

Ten Ancient Scrolls

Tom Hopkins

A s I began the exciting journey of reading the scrolls nearly 30 years ago, it was obvious I had found a source of strength and the key to unlock my potential and fulfill my dreams. The message of each scroll still touches my heart each time I read them. I repeat the message from Scroll III—"I will persist until I succeed "—in this manner daily: failure will never overtake me if my determination to succeed is strong enough. *The Greatest Salesman in the World* is truly an inspired writing and may the message not die with the messenger. I give thanks daily to Og for having such a tremendous affect on my life and now on the lives of those I am blessed to teach.

The 6th Emotions Scroll

*T*oday I will be master of my emotions.

The tides advance; the tides recede. Winter goes and summer comes. Summer wanes and the cold increases. The sun rises; the sun sets. The moon is full; the moon is black. The birds arrive; the birds depart. Flowers bloom; flowers fade. Seeds are sown; harvests are reaped. **All nature is a circle of moods and I am a part of nature and so, like the tides, my moods will rise; my moods will fall.**

Today I will be master of my emotions.

It is one of nature's tricks, little understood, that each day I awaken with moods that have changed from yesterday. Yesterday's joy will become today's sadness; yet today's sadness will grow into tomorrow's joy. Inside me is a wheel, constantly turning from sadness to joy, from exultation to depression, from happiness to melancholy. Like the flowers, today's full bloom of joy will fade and wither into despondency, yet I will remember that as today's dead flower carries the seed of tomorrow's bloom so, too, does today's sadness carry the seed of tomorrow's joy.

Today I will be master of my emotions.

And how will I master these emotions so that each day will be productive? For unless my mood is right the day will be a failure. Trees and plants depend on the weather to flourish but I make my own weather, yea I transport it with me. If I bring rain and gloom and darkness and pessimism to my customers then they will react with rain and gloom and darkness and pessimism and they will purchase naught. **If I bring joy and enthusiasm and brightness and laughter to my customers they will react with joy and enthusiasm and brightness and laughter and my weather will produce a harvest of sales and a granary of gold for me.**

Today I will be master of my emotions.

And how will I master my emotions so that every day is a happy day, and a productive one? I will learn this secret of the ages: **Weak is he who permits his thoughts to control his actions; strong is he who forces his actions to control his thoughts.** Each day, when I awaken, I will follow this plan of battle before I am captured by the forces of sadness, self-pity and failure capture me:

If I feel depressed I will sing.

If I feel sad I will laugh.

If I feel ill I will double my labor.

If I feel fear I will plunge ahead.

If I feel inferior I will wear new garments.

If I feel uncertain I will raise my voice.

If I feel poverty I will think of wealth to come.

If I feel incompetent I will remember past success.

If I feel insignificant I will remember my goals.

Today I will be master of my emotions.

Henceforth, I will know that only those with inferior ability can always be at their best, and I am not inferior. **There will be days when I must constantly struggle against forces that would tear me down. Those such as despair and sadness are simple to recognize but there are others that approach with a smile and the hand of friendship and they can also destroy me.** Against them, too, I must never relinquish control.

If I become overconfident I will recall my failures.

If I overindulge I will think of past hungers.

If I feel complacency I will remember my competition.

If I enjoy moments of greatness I will remember moments of shame.

If I feel all-powerful I will try to stop the wind.

If I attain great wealth I will remember one unfed mouth.

If I become overly proud I will remember a moment of weakness.

If I feel my skill is unmatched I will look at the stars.

Today I will be master of my emotions.

And with this new knowledge I will also understand and recognize the moods of him on whom I call. **I will make allowances for his anger and irritation of today for he knows not the secret of controlling his mind. I can withstand his arrows and insults for now I know that tomorrow he will change and be a joy to approach.**

No longer will I judge a man on one meeting; no longer will I fail to call again tomorrow on he who meets me with hate today. This day he will not buy gold chariots for a penny, yet tomorrow he would exchange his home for a tree. My knowledge of this secret will be my key to great wealth.

Today I will be master of my emotions.

Henceforth I will recognize and identify the mystery of moods in all mankind, and in me. From this moment I am prepared to control whatever personality awakes in me each day. **I will master my moods through positive action and when I master my moods I will control my destiny.**

Today I control my destiny, and my destiny is to become The Greatest Salesman in the World!

I will become master of myself.

I will become great.

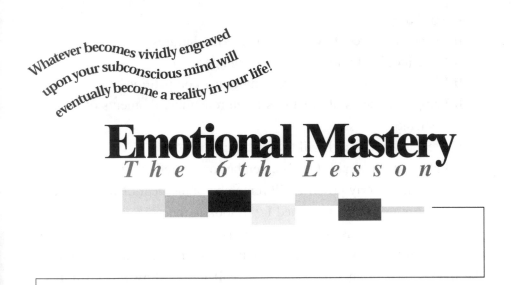

Whatever becomes vividly engraved upon your subconscious mind will eventually become a reality in your life!

Emotional Mastery
T h e 6 t h L e s s o n

S ales often requires direct contact with people; therefore, it is important that you understand human nature in order to become successful. Perhaps one of the most difficult things to understand is human emotion.

Both internal and external forces trigger emotion. This makes it difficult to pinpoint your prospect's emotional state. To deal with people more effectively, you must not only understand their emotions, but your own as well.

The sixth scroll will help you gain a clearer understanding of how emotions operate. In this scroll you will discover underlying emotional triggers that will allow you to control their emotions and help neutralize harmful emotions in yourself and your prospects.

1 | The Two Sides of Nature

"All nature is a circle of moods and I am a part of nature and so, like the tides my moods will rise and my moods will fall."

It is amazing how we observe nature, yet never fully understand how it affects us. And the atom, the smallest building block of matter, testifies to the existence of two sides of nature: positive and negative. Likewise, there are positive and negative forces around us constantly. Sometimes we are moved by these forces, like a fragile leaf blown about by the wind. Yet, the reality is that we possess the power to move these positive and negative forces as if the forces were the leaves and we were the wind.

In every opposition there is the seed of an equivalent benefit. If you can identify that benefit, you can remain emotionally balanced, regardless of whether your emotional tide rises or falls. In the words of The Scroll Marked II, "You can love the light, for it shows you the way, yet you can also love the darkness, for it shows you the stars."

2 | Understanding Mood Swings

"It is one of nature's tricks little understood, that each day I awaken with moods that have changed from yesterday."

It has been said that the deeper the sorrow people experience, the greater is their capacity for joy. Moods are like the multitude of colors in a rainbow; each hue triggers a different sensation within us, and each mood we experience adds a different flavor to the taste of life.

If our moods were always the same, life would be boring. Because your moods often change from day to day, you have to learn to control them. After all, life is like a roller coaster ride, and how you control or fail to control your moods can determine whether the ride is a terrifying experience or an exhilarating adventure.

3 | The Atmosphere Which Yields Success

"If I bring joy and enthusiasm and brightness and laughter to my customers they will react with joy and enthusiasm and brightness and laughter and my weather will produce a harvest of sales and a granary of gold for me."

Negative emotions should never carry over into your contact with others. They are like a foul odor; if you carry them with you, people will be offended and won't want to do business with you. Cleanse yourself of these negative emotions; bathe yourself in more positive emotions.

Sales people often walk into an atmosphere not conducive to the sales transaction. For example, your prospect may be depressed because his business is slow or because some tragedy just occurred in his personal life. Rather than change the atmosphere, you might allow the atmosphere to affect you and end up leaving without the sale. You have it within your power to change the atmosphere; so change it.

4 | Proactive Thought Control

"Weak is he who permits his thoughts to control his actions; strong is he who forces his actions to control his thoughts."

Here is an age-old secret: Actions are dictated by their thoughts and emotions. Some people allow these thoughts and emotions to determine their actions even when their actions become non-productive. Thoughts are like dreams or nightmares; just because you have them, does not mean they will come true. Choose the thoughts you will act on, just as you choose the dreams you will pursue.

Instead, if you use your actions to trigger your thoughts, you will exercise greater control over your mental machinery and direct the thoughts and actions that will carry you closer to your goals. For instance, every salesperson likes to meet a prospect who is eager to buy. Try acting as if your next sales call is an eager prospect and see how your behavior influences the sale.

5 | Counteracting Emotional Lows
"There will be days when I must constantly struggle against forces, which would tear me down."

Watch any child learning to ride a bicycle and you will observe a very simple yet powerful principle. He begins wobbling along, leaning too far to one side, until he eventually loses his balance. Training wheels make it more difficult to fall, but he still leans, dependent now on the training wheels, until he finally discovers the art of balance and can ride without either wheel touching the ground.

Our mood swings operate very much in the same way. If you swing too far to one side you are sure to experience a painful emotional fall. There are many simple things you can do to counteract emotional lows and keep yourself balanced: If you find yourself overtaken by sadness, see a comedy or do something to make someone else laugh. When you are afraid, do the thing you fear and you will destroy the fear. In other words, do something that will lean you in the opposite direction and keep you emotionally balanced.

6 | Counteracting Emotional Highs
"Those such as despair and sadness are simple to recognize but there are others which approach with a smile and a hand of friendship and they can also destroy me."

The most common form of emotional imbalance is the emotional low. This is why we see so many ads for the treatment of depression. However, the emotional high can be just as destructive, and even more dangerous, because it often goes undetected and therefore, untreated.

Egomaniacs and power hungry fanatics are as emotionally out of balance as someone who is manic depressive or suffering from low self-esteem. Here are a few simple suggestions for counteracting emotional highs: When you become successful, take time out to visit those less fortunate than yourself. When you're having dinner at your favorite restaurant or taking a vacation, remember a time in your life when things were not so easy and count your blessings. Whenever you begin to feel invincible, simply review your last will and testament, if you have one. If you don't, then prepare one and remind yourself just how frail life can be.

7 | Tolerance for Moody People
"I will make allowances for his anger and irritation of today for he knows not the secret of controlling his mind."

Although you may have mastered your emotions, most people probably have not. The awareness that some of your prospects have little or no control over their emotions should give you a greater tolerance for their mood swings. Becoming offended by moody and irritable people will only cause you to lose your patience, your temper, and ultimately the sale. Rather than take offense, be understanding, patient, and try to set a positive emotional tone to cut through the tension.

8 | Immunity to Rejection
"I can withstand his arrows and insults for now for I know that tomorrow he will change and be a joy to approach."

Taking offense to rejection is a clear sign of personal insecurity, so don't take it personally if someone neglects to accept your offer. After all, he is merely rejecting your offer, not you as a person.

After you have made every effort to address his objections and he still chooses to decline, try to leave him with a positive impression. He may develop an interest later, and if you have made a positive impression, you also will have made the sale.

The secret to becoming immune to rejection is this: Remember that every action produces a reaction. If the reaction you get is not what you want, simply try a different action until you get the desired results. Rejection only stings if you believe your efforts have failed. But if the aim of your efforts is simply to produce a reaction, then you can never fail.

9 | Secret Key to Great Wealth

"No longer will I judge a man on one meeting; no longer will I fail to call again tomorrow on him who meets me with hate today."

You are not the same person you were five years ago, five days ago or even five minutes ago. Time has a way of changing you physically, mentally and emotionally. But although first impressions are powerful impressions, they are not cast in stone.

There are a countless number of variables that could turn today's pessimistic prospect into tomorrow's profitable customer. A life insurance salesperson may not make it to first base with a young executive in his prime. However, tonight a close family member may die, and tomorrow that same young executive may have a whole new perspective on the value of life insurance. Don't be afraid to call again a person who at one time was not too receptive.

10 | Mastering Moods Skillfully
"I will master my moods through positive action and when I master my moods I will control my destiny."

Life is not a game of chance. Destiny does not bless some with happiness while it curses others with sadness. You have always possessed the ability to control the results you produce in life, yet with the knowledge of how to control your emotions, you can dramatically increase your productivity.

To be a true master, you must continue to develop your skill through consistent practice. Practice controlling your emotions and provoking positive emotions in others. Use the mood control strategies you have observed in the 6th Scroll and throughout this chapter. Apply these ideas at home, at work and even at play until they become a standard part of your everyday life.

! | Developing Emotions: A Practical Exercise

Here is a simple exercise you can perform to help you master your emotions. It was originally developed by Benjamin Franklin to help him improve his personality. As one of the founding fathers of America, Mr. Franklin was a highly visible public figure. On occasion, he noticed that his temper and bluntness created friction in his relationships with others. So, being a prudent man, he devised a simple, yet scientific, method for correcting the flaws he observed in his character.

Franklin compiled a list of moral virtues he had learned about during the course of his studies. Included in the list were qualities such as temperance, silence, order, resolution, frugality, industry, sincerity, justice, moderation, cleanliness, tranquility, chastity, and humility. He resolved to build these virtues into his own personality. However, in his initial attempt, he found the task to be quite difficult. While he worked to guard against one fault, another would pop up and take him by surprise.

So he decided to take the rifle approach and focus on one fault at a time instead of using the shotgun approach, in which he attempted to correct many faults at once. Instead of trying to be completely virtuous, he directed his energies to becoming virtuous a little at a time.

He began a little book in which he devoted one page to the development of each virtue. He made seven columns on the page—one for each day of the week. Along the left side of the page he listed an abbreviation for each of the thirteen virtues and drew a line to create a row for each. Next he wrote at the top of the page the specific virtue he would concentrate on during the week. As the week progressed he placed a mark in the appropriate column and row each time he found himself faltering in any one of the areas listed. His objective was to keep the row of the focused virtue free of marks. This enhanced awareness of his conduct and helped him target and eliminate undesirable behavior.

Use the Franklin method as your exercise for this chapter. Make a list of the personal qualities you want to improve. Identify one quality from the list that you will concentrate on during the week. Make a written note each time you find yourself faltering in another area on your list. Each week address a different personal quality until you have improved in every area on your list. After you have completed the list, simply start the process over again. Feel free to add other qualities you need to improve.

Amazingly enough as you learn to master your own emotions, influencing the emotions of others will become quite easy. To provoke a particular emotional response in someone else, all you need to do is supply the identical emotional stimulus — you will reap what you sow. For instance, if you want to reap happiness, simply plant happiness.

Charles Jones

Publisher • Motivator • Humorist

*C*harlie Jones entered the field of selling at the age of six. He sold *Liberty* and *Collier* magazines and received numerous awards before moving up to his own Kool–Aid and ice cream business at age eight.

He entered the insurance business at age 22, with one of America's Top Ten companies. At age 23, he was awarded his agency's Most Valuable Associate award. Ten years later he received his company's highest management award for recruiting, manpower and development, and business management. At age 37, his organization exceeded $100,000,000 in force, at which time he founded Life Management Services to share his experiences through seminars and consulting services.

For over a quarter of a century, thousands of audiences in America, Canada, Mexico, Australia, New Zealand, Europe and Asia have experienced nonstop laughter as Mr. "T" shared his ideas about life's most challenging situations in business and at home.

He is the author of, *Life is Tremendous—7 Laws of Leadership*, with more than 1,000,000 copies in print, and two of his speeches, *The Price of Leadership* and *Where Does Leadership Begin?* have been enjoyed

by millions on record and cassette, and at conventions.

He is featured in the *Dynamic Achievers World Network* television series, the *Automotive Sales Training Network* satellite training service, *Insights Into Excellence* video training series, Nightingale's *Executive Treasury of Humor* cassette series and two 30-minutes color films, *The Leading Edge and Learning –A Tremendous Experience.* The films have been used by more than 1,000 companies throughout the free world.

He is the president of Life Management Services, Inc.; Executive Books; and a member of the prestigious speakers Roundtable. The recipient of the CPAE Award for speaking skills and professionalism from the National Speakers Association, he is also a member of West Shore Chamber of Commerce, the National Speakers Association, the International Platform Association, and the Gideons and Christian Businessmen's Committee. His list of credits also includes a past direc torship of Harrisburg Association of Life Underwriters, and Chairman of the Pennsylvania Association of Life Underwriters-Awards Committee and Sales Congress.

! • | Discovering the Secrets of the Successful

How did you get started in the field of sales?
At the age of seven I would stop people and sell them on the idea of listening to me yodel. They would pay me two cents for the privilege of not hearing me yodel. After that I started selling magazines for a nickel and I earned a penny commission. Then I moved up to selling the Saturday Evening Post for a dime with a whopping two-cent commission. At the age of twelve I started selling popsicles. I would buy the popsicles in bulk for four cents apiece and sell them for ten cents apiece generating about a couple of dollars a day, which at the time was considered a lot of money. As a teenager I loved clothes so I started selling men's clothes in a department store and loved it. I became so good at it that a young lady in another department told her husband about me and he came down to the store to ask me if I would be interested in selling life insurance. At first I had no interest in it whatsoever until the man told me that he would train me and pay me the same thing I was presently earning. When I finally realized what life insurance really did and discovered that the commission on selling one policy was three times as much as I would make in a week, I thought "this is too good to be true." After I got into the insurance business I was a lousy insurance sales person but I was a great recruiter. After telling others how great the insurance business was I not only convinced them to get involved but I also convinced myself to stay in the business instead of giving up.

What is the greatest challenge you have had to face over the years?
I was born in the twenties and as a child my mother left us a few times then by the age of twelve her and my father got divorced. Because of the poverty and lacking a real home life I decided to run away from home at the age of fifteen. So I dropped out of high school and never attended college, therefore I would say that my greatest challenge was that fear that I never received any formal education.

What do you consider to be the most outstanding achievement of your career?
Obtaining a personal relationship with Jesus Christ that completely transformed my life and developing an insatiable love for reading.

Who were some of your most influential role models and mentors?
I met one of my most influential role models when I was 6 years old at Sunday school. His name was George Mowery and he was my Sunday school teacher. George Mowery was a 21 years old shoe salesman and he always drove a new car. He always took us places, he took us fishing, swimming and to his home. He paid me a nickel to memorize bible verses. Most of my life has been lived in the image of George Mowery. I have tried to be as much of a mentor to children as George Mowery was to me. After I became an insurance salesman Jim Rudisil became a great role model for me. Jim was the president of the Chamber of Commerce and the president of the Christians businessman association. Jim was a great speaker, but more important he was a godly man. I had never known that a man could be godly and such a financial success and respected in the community. Hal Nut who was the director of insurance marketing at Perdue University was my greatest speaking role model. I became so taken by Hal's uninhibited enthusiasm that over the years I became just like him in my presentation style. When I entered into the speaking arena books became my mentors. I read great authors like Watchman Nee, Oswald Chambers, Charles Spurgeon, A.W. Tozer and other greats.

What is the most effective sales technique you have ever used?
First you must have a good approach, then you have to point out a general problem that we all have, then you point out a specific problem that they have, then point out the solution to the problem. To close the sale you need to use some form of motivation to loosen up the prospect and then you need to give him at least six opportunities to say yes. The strategy works but what really sells are stories that help him see his need to your solution.

Give an example of how you would use this technique in a real life situation?

In the insurance business I have often told the story about two kinds of dads. I would say that there is the see kind of dad and then there is the have kind of dad. Now the see kind of dad says "I am going to see that my children have every thing that they need as long as I am here to see it". But the have kind of dad says that "I want my children to have every thing I can give them, whether I am here to see it or not, so I am going to buy a lot of insurance." Over the years, this simple story has inspired many people to buy insurance.

What is the best advice that you can offer an aspiring salesperson?

Over the years I have had many salespeople come to me for advice even when I was an aspiring salesperson myself. So I developed two kinds of advice, good advice and priceless advice. Now my good advice would be good but my priceless advice would be better. My priceless advice was, never take advice, just learn the fundamentals of your business and practice them on a regular basis. Knowing your own business and being prepared gives you the confidence you will need to succeed. Knowing your business will give you head knowledge but to gain the heart knowledge that you will need to keep from giving up when the going gets rough you should read the biographies of great people and see the many trials they went through before they succeeded.

If you have not always lived by your current philosophy what provoked the change?

During the early part of my life till I was 22 years old I was the complete opposite from what I am now. I was profane and obscene because it was popular to be that way in the circles that I traveled in. At that time my philosophy was to do unto others before they do unto you. But then I came to realize that there were two different worlds. I wanted to be a part of the world that practiced discipline, truth, giving sharing and serving. So I decided to adopt that philosophy of good, I eventually became a husband and a father. Then one day an old friend told me about Jesus, since then my life has never been the same. My friend never once argued with me but he would have me to look up verses and ask me to explain what they meant. By doing this he caused me to realize the depth of Gods love for me and that changed my life forever.

Ten Ancient Scrolls

Charles Jones

O g Mandino will always be the greatest salesman in the world, because his scrolls have sold and inspired millions around the world to live and practice the principles that bring true success. These ten laws of success become more meaningful with every reading. They will be as fresh one hundred years from now as they are today. Anyone who commits the scrolls to memory will become a source of wisdom for all you meet.

The 7th Humor Scroll

I will laugh at the world. No living creature can laugh except man. Trees may bleed when they are wounded, and beasts in the field will cry in pain and hunger, yet only I have the gift of laughter and it is mine to use whenever I choose. Henceforth I will cultivate the habit of laughter.

I will smile and my digestion will improve; I will chuckle and my burdens will be lightened; I will laugh and my life will be lengthened for this is the great secret of long life and now it is mine.

I will laugh at the world. **And most of all, I will laugh at myself for man is most comical when he takes himself too seriously.** Never will I fall into this trap of the mind. For though I be nature's greatest miracle am I not still a mere grain tossed about by the winds of time? Do I truly know whence I came or whither I am bound? Will my concern for this day not seem foolish ten years hence? **Why should I permit the petty happenings of today to disturb me? What can take place before this sun sets which will not seem insignificant in the river of centuries?**

I will laugh at the world. And how can I laugh when confronted with man or deed, which offends me so as to bring forth my tears or my curses? **Four words I will train myself to say until they become a habit so strong that immediately they will appear in my mind whenever good humor threatens to depart from me.** These words, passed down from the ancients, will carry me through every adversity and maintain my life in balance. These four words are: This too shall pass.

I will laugh at the world. For all worldly things shall indeed pass. When I am heavy with heartache I shall console myself that this too shall pass; when I am puffed with success I shall warn myself that this too shall pass. When I am strangled in poverty I shall tell myself that this too shall pass; when I am burdened with wealth I shall tell myself that this too shall pass. Yea, verily, where is he who built the pyramid? Is he not buried within its stone? And will the pyramid, one day, not also be buried under sand? If all things shall pass why should I be of concern for today?

I will laugh at the world. I will paint this day with laughter; I will frame this night in song. **Never will I labor to be happy; rather will I remain too busy to be sad. I will enjoy today's happiness today.** It is not grain to be stored in a box. It is not wine to be saved in a jar. It cannot be saved for the morrow. It must be sown and reaped on the same day and this I will do, henceforth.

I will laugh at the world. **And with my laughter all things will be reduced to their proper size.** I will laugh at my failures and they will vanish in clouds of new dreams; I will laugh at my successes and they will shrink to their true value. I will laugh at evil and it will die untasted; I will laugh at goodness and it will thrive and abound. **Each day will be triumphant only when my smiles bring forth smiles from others and this I do in selfishness, for those on whom I frown are those who purchase not my goods.**

I will laugh at the world. **Henceforth will I shed only tears of sweat, for those of sadness or remorse or frustration are of no value in the market place whilst each smile can be exchanged for gold and each kind word, spoken from my heart, can build a castle.**

Never will I allow myself to become so important, so wise, so dignified, so powerful, that I forget how to laugh at myself and my world. In this matter **I will always remain as a child, for only as a child am I given the ability to look up to others;** and so long as I look up to another I will never grow too long for my cot.

I will laugh at the world. And so long as I can laugh never will I be poor. This, then, is one of nature's greatest gifts, and I will waste it no more. Only with laughter and happiness can I truly become a success. Only with laughter and happiness can I enjoy the fruits of my labor. Were it not so, far better would it be to fail, for happiness is the wine that sharpens the taste of the meal. **To enjoy success I must have happiness, and laughter will be the maiden who serves me.**

I will be happy.

I will be successful. I will be the greatest salesman the world has ever known.

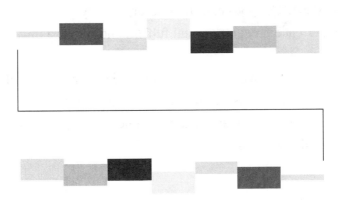

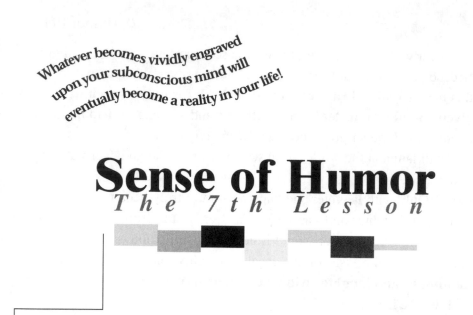

Whatever becomes vividly engraved upon your subconscious mind will eventually become a reality in your life!

Sense of Humor
The 7th Lesson

A sense of humor is not usually considered an important professional tool unless you are a comedian. However, humor is an asset in any profession. In the sales profession a sense of humor is as important to the salesperson as a whip is to the lion tamer.

Humor is more than having the ability to tell a joke. A sense of humor, like happiness, is a state of mind, an attitude that can be cultivated by anyone. As you learn how to enhance your sense of humor you will experience greater personal fulfillment by spreading joy in the lives of others.

The seventh scroll will show you how to develop a sense of humor. Even more important, this scroll will prove that the treasure of happiness is more valuable than any material riches, and that humor is a key to accessing this priceless treasure.

1 | Laughter Effects Physical Conditions

"I will smile and my digestion will improve; I will chuckle and my burdens will be lightened; I will laugh and my life will be lengthened for this is the secret of long life and now it is mine."

Long ago, one of the wisest men ever known discovered something that modern man is just beginning to understand. The great King Solomon said, "A merry heart doeth good like a medicine" (Proverbs 17:22). Recently, The American Heart Association confirmed that Solomon's wisdom continues to hold true today.

In 1998, they released information from a study revealing that freedom from stress and anxiety contributes more to a healthy heart than mere exercise and the avoidance of unhealthy foods. Maintaining a good sense of humor is important because it frees you from stress and anxiety.

What does one's physical condition have to do with sales? Ob-viously, if you are not physically healthy, you can't generate the energy and enthusiasm that is such an important part of the sales process.

2 | The Ability to Laugh at Yourself

"And most of all, I will laugh at myself for man is most comical when he takes himself too seriously."

The ability to laugh at your blunders is proof that you accept your humanity. It is also a clear sign that you can be forgiving of yourself and thus maintain one of the most important relationships in the world, your relationship with you.

Since mistakes are an unavoidable part of the process, you can't take them too seriously. If you learn to laugh at your mistakes, you will enjoy every step of the journey to your destiny—even the clumsy ones.

3 | Laughing in the Face of Adversity

"Why should I permit the petty happening of today to disturb me? What can take place before the sun sets that will not seem insignificant in the rivers of centuries?"

Laughing in the face of adversity puts it into perspective. Imagine someone trying to intimidate you. Nothing would give him greater pleasure than seeing you sweat and crumble under the pressure. However, if you were to react with laughter, he would be disarmed and the effects would be weakened. Laughter takes the teeth out of adversity and removes its power to intimidate you.

4 | This-Too-Shall-Pass

"Four words will I train myself to say until they become a habit so strong that immediately they will appear in my mind whenever good humor threatens to depart from me."

These four simple words can enable you to maintain a positive and productive attitude regardless of what throws your life out of balance. Every experience we encounter is only temporary.

Let's say that a salesman finds himself in a rut. He feels depressed because his sales are down, so he carries his depression with him to his next appointment and continues to perpetuate his losing streak. The more depressed he feels, the deeper his rut becomes. It becomes a Catch-22 situation, he's depressed because he's in a rut, and he's in a rut because he's depressed. The only way to break this endless downward cycle is for him to realize that this-too-shall-pass.

5 | Stay too Busy to be Sad
"Never will I labor to be happy; rather I will remain too busy to be sad. I will enjoy today's happiness today."

Sadness is only felt when the mind is engaged in negative thought. Engage your mind with thoughts about positive experiences, and talk about your greatest joys. You will soon discover that there is little time remaining for you to wallow in sorrow.

6 | Laughter Puts Things into Perspective
"And with my laughter all things will be reduced to their proper size."

It's important to keep things in their proper perspective. Becoming too pompous and proud of your success can be as detrimental as becoming too saddened by your failure. However, be willing to laugh at your success, realizing that it can be temporary; and be willing to laugh at your failure, too, since it can be just as temporary.

7 | The Selfish Use of Laughter
"Each day will be triumphant only when my smiles bring forth smiles from others and this I do in selfishness, for those on whom I frown are those who purchase not my goods."

Spreading laughter and happiness into the lives of others can be very rewarding. Often, people fail to bring joy to others because they don't see what's in it for them. Yet, in the sales profession there is a very good reason why you should not only learn to laugh, but learn to make others laugh as well. The reason is this: People like to do business with people they like, and they like people who make them happy.

Laughter, like a yawn, is often contagious. Smile and others will smile with you. When you smile, you give off positive energy that compels others to smile back. You need not understand how this works; you just need to understand that it works, and then use it to your own benefit. Try it. Smile at others during the course of the day and watch them throw back a smile almost as if it were an unconscious reflex action.

When you share a smile or laughter, you neutralize their defenses. People often become defensive with salespeople. When you exchange a smile with them, you establish a slight degree of rapport and slip past the first phase of their consumer defense mechanism. If you continue to develop this rapport, you increase the chance that they will buy what you have to offer.

8 | Exchanging Smiles for Gold

"I will shed only tears of sweat, for those of sadness or remorse or frustration are of no value in the marketplace whilst each smile can be exchanged for gold and each kind word, spoken from the heart can build a castle."

Since happiness is one of life's most sought after treasures, whenever you give it to someone, you have given him or her a precious gift. Most people can detect when you're not being sincere. As a legitimate sales person you must never engage in a transaction that is not in the best interest of your customer. Therefore, even though your smiles inspire others to cooperate with you, you must still provide them with a product or service that is of genuine value.

9 | Remaining as a Child

"I will always remain as a child for only as a child am I given the ability to look up to others."

Take time to notice the laughter of children. They have the rare talent to find great joy in the most insignificant things. They have a natural ability to enjoy life because they have not yet learned of all the fears and limitations which plague adults. It is in this state of childlike innocence that we can find happiness easily and enjoy it abundantly.

Remaining as a child keeps us from losing the wonder of curiosity, the magic of imagination and the ability to grow. Living life as a child is not only a practical way to experience a more fulfilling life, it is the only way to enter into that heavenly state of eternal bliss.

10 | Success without Happiness

"To enjoy success I must have happiness, and laughter will be the maiden who serves me."

Viewing a rainbow without color, smelling a flower without fragrance and tasting food without flavor are all as unfulfilling as achieving success without happiness. If you owned the entire world and everything in it, but lacked happiness, you would still be poor. Yet, if you had no possession on earth other than happiness, you would be very rich.

In your professional pursuits you should not lose sight of the object of your quest. Remember, if the rewards you receive for your efforts are only those in your paycheck, then you are terribly underpaid. However, if happiness is indeed the pot of gold at the end of your professional rainbow, then you have it within your own power to make every day payday.

! | Developing Laughter:
• | A Practical Exercise

The following exercise will help you learn to use your sense of humor more effectively in the sales process. If you see yourself as being a little dry in the humor department, this exercise will serve a dual purpose for you. Not only will it enhance your persuasiveness in sales; it will also add more flavor to other areas of your life.

One of the most important, yet frequently ignored, steps in the sales process is neutralizing the mind of the prospect. Neutralizing the prospect involves penetrating his or her consumer defense system and establishing enough rapport to make him receptive to your offer. This step is vitally important because, unless you first neutralize the prospects, their minds may not be open to even considering your offer.

Often the sales person is so caught up in making the sale that he completely forgets a very basic principle: If in your initial contact, you do not immediately address something of interest, then you are nothing more than an interruption in their lives. Memorize this simple idea and think about it before you approach any prospect. The following are seven methods for neutralizing the prospect:

1. Share laughter through a joke, a story, or just a facial expression.
2. Give them complements on their appearance or personal traits; be sincere, however.
3. Mention a mutual friend or acquaintance, but never in a gossiping manner.
4. Discuss a mutual point of interest you both enjoy, such as work or hobbies.
5. Seek their opinion about your product, service or anything else.
6. Ask them a question, then sincerely listen to the answer.
7. Give them a gift or sample that does not put them under any obligation.

To help you strengthen your sense of humor, practice looking for the humor in the situations you encounter each day. Look for the bright side of every circumstance and you will soon discover that the bright side becomes a lot more obvious to your view. It will also be helpful to practice the following methods of tickling your prospects.

1. Grin ever so casually to set a tone of lightness in the atmosphere.
2. Smile with full teeth and eyes to always trigger a smile in return.
3. Look at facial expressions and body language to indicate when laughter is about to break.
4. Chuckle before you begin laughing (starting with a full laugh may startle them).
5. Use a friendly touch on the hand or shoulder (use discretion with direct physical contact).
6. Use a soft tone of voice to prospects and make them feel more at ease.

S p o t l i g h t   o n :

Paul J. Meyer

Author • Entrepreneur •
Philanthropist

Paul J. Meyer was in his mid twenties and a top sales agent for National Union Life Insurance when he stepped into the home office in Florida one spring morning and found the place completely empty. Furniture, typewriters, filing cabinets—everything—had vanished. Even the carpet was gone. After making a few calls Paul discovered that the company's founder had moved the entire company out of state over the weekend to avoid being shut down by the Insurance Commission for some questionable business dealings. Though he could have walked away from this fiasco, Paul Meyer's personal integrity compelled him to shoulder the responsibility and put every thing he had on the line to pay off creditors, cover policyholder investments and find new positions for his staff. It is that kind of integrity that is one of the cornerstones of Mr. Meyer's success.

Paul J. Meyer became interested at an early age in the principles of individual growth, development, and success. He applied what he learned about success through goal setting to his chosen career of professional sales, and became a millionaire by the age of twenty-seven. He soon moved into sales management and began to teach success principles to the members of his organization.

For approximately four decades, Paul J. Meyer has been one of the most celebrated leaders in the field of personal and professional development. It has been said that Meyer's pioneering efforts made him the catalyst of the modern self-improvement industry. Generating more than $2 billion in revenue from his time-proven training materials, books, and recordings, Meyer has sold more materials than any other self-improvement author. He has been quoted and featured by more than one hundred authors in their own books, and has received awards from civic and business organizations all over the world.

His full-length programs are sold in 60 countries worldwide and in 17 languages, with other translations in preparation. Meyer's uniquely positive view of the world ranks him, along with other "greats" like Og Mandino, as one of the most renowned masters of all time in sales and sales management training.

Meyer has also been called the "ultimate entrepreneur." In addition to creating his flagship company, Success Motivation Institute, Inc., Meyer is the founder of Leadership Management International, Inc., and owner of nearly 40 other companies.

He has created a family enterprise that spans the worlds of publishing, education, finance, insurance, real estate, manufacturing, and much, much more. Recent books by Paul Meyer include *I Inherited A Fortune* and *Bridging The Leadership Gap*.

! • | Discovering the Secrets of the Successful

How did you get started in the field of sales?

My first remembrance of selling was when I was about 12 years old, and I sold magazines door-to-door, including *Ladies Home Journal,* etc. I won several national awards. I liked working with magazines; I liked interacting with the women; and they liked me. That was my first wonderful taste of selling.

As a teenager I bought old bicycles and reworked them and sold them. I also enjoyed selling fruit that I had friends picking from the orchard and then we got organized and I had them selling fruit along the highway.

At age 19, I began selling insurance in Columbus, Georgia. I set a national record for that company the very first year. If I hadn't already been hooked on selling, that experience would have done it. I loved helping people and selling them something that would really help them.

What is the greatest challenge you have had to face over the years?

Putting up with negative people and people who look for ways that things can't be done and don't mind telling everybody. I do not like to have to tolerate restricting my own resourcefulness, innovativeness, creativity, etc. Nor do I like negative people doing that to other people.

What do you consider to be the most outstanding achievement of your career?

Starting Success Motivation Institute, Inc. and being at the forefront of the entire personal achievement industry. In addition, it was a great thrill being the author of the industry's best-selling programs. It is satisfying achievement to me to have affiliated companies in addition to th original company having sold more personal achievement products than any other affiliated companies.

Who were some of you most influential role models and mentors?
Jesus Christ is my foremost role model. Next comes my parents—my mother and father. In addition, some special teachers, including my first-grade teacher Mrs. McCormick.

What is the most effective sales technique you have ever used?
Having a servant's attitude, a servant's consciousness, a servant's awareness. Loving people unconditionally.

Given an example of how you would apply this technique in a real life situation?
Ask questions and be a good listener to find out what prospective clients need. Then ask questions to how best to meet that need.

What is the most valuable advice you can offer to an aspiring salesperson?
Learn the basics of your business, be patient, build your career solidly one step at a time, study the top sales producers in your organization and see what makes them successful, stay focused and be persistent.

If you have not always lived by your current philosophy, what provoked the change?
My life documents the fact that I have nearly always lived by my current philosophy.

Ten Ancient Scrolls
Paul J. Meyer _____

I have read almost every book written on salesmanship. Og
Mandino has distilled the wisdom of them all in *The Greatest
Salesman in the World.* No one who follows the selling principles
expressed in the ten ancient scrolls will ever fail, and no one will ever
be truly great without them. But the author has done more than present
the principles—he has woven them into the fabric of one of the most
fascinating stories I've ever read."

*Paul J. Meyer maintains that the ten ancient scrolls are as valid to
today as they were when he first read them following their 1968 publication; and the spirit of integrity they capture is needed more than ever.*

The *8th* Progress
Scroll

*T*oday I will multiply my value a hundredfold.
A mulberry leaf touched with the genius of man becomes silk.

A field of clay touched with the genius of man becomes a castle.

A Cyprus tree touched with the genius of man becomes a shrine. A cut of sheep's hair touched with the genius of man becomes raiment for a king.

If it is possible for leaves and clay and wood and hair to have their value multiplied a hundred, yea a thousandfold by man, cannot I do the same with the clay, which bears my name?

Today I will multiply my value a hundredfold. **I am likened to a grain of wheat** which faces one of three futures. The wheat can be placed in a sack and dumped in a stall until it is fed to swine. Or it can be ground to flour and made into bread. Or it can be placed in the earth and allowed to grow until its golden head divides and produces a thousand grains from the one.

I am likened to a grain of wheat with one difference. The wheat cannot choose whether it be fed to swine, ground for bread, or planted to multiply. I have a choice and I will not let my life be fed to swine nor will I let it be ground under the rocks of failure and despair to be broken open and devoured by the will of others.

Today I will multiply my value a hundredfold.

To grow and multiply it is necessary to plant the wheat grain in the darkness of the earth and my failures, my despairs, my ignorance, and my inabilities are the darkness in which I have been planted in order to ripen. Now, **like the wheat grain which will sprout and blossom only if it is nurtured with rain and sun and warm winds, I too must nurture my body and mind to fulfill my dreams.** But to grow to full stature the wheat must wait on the whims of nature. I need not wait for I have the power to choose my own destiny.

Today I will multiply my value a hundredfold.

And how will I accomplish this? **First I will set goals for the day, the week, the month, the year, and my life.** Just as the rain must fall before the wheat will crack its shell and sprout, so must I have objectives before my life will crystallize. In setting my goals I will consider my best performance of the past and multiply it a hundredfold. This will be the standard by which I will live in the future. Never will I be of concern that my goals are too high for is it not better to aim my spear at the moon and strike only an eagle than to aim my spear at the eagle and strike only a rock?

Today I will multiply my value a hundredfold.

The height of my goals will not hold me in awe though I may stumble often before they are reached. If I stumble I will rise and my falls will not concern me for all men must stumble often to reach the hearth. Only a worm is free from the worry of stumbling. I am not a worm. I am not an onion plant. I am not a sheep. I am a man. Let others build a cave with their clay. I will build a castle with mine.

Today I will multiply my value a hundredfold.

And just as the sun must warm the earth to bring forth the seedling of wheat so, too, will the words on these scrolls warm my life and turn my dreams into reality.

Today I will surpass every action, which I performed yesterday. I will climb today's mountain to the utmost of my ability yet tomorrow I will climb higher than today, and the next will be higher than tomorrow. **To surpass the deeds of others is unimportant; to surpass my own deeds is all.**

Today I will multiply my value a hundredfold.

And just as the warm wind guides the wheat to maturity, the same winds will carry my voice to those who will listen and my words will announce my goals. Once spoken I dare not recall them lest I lose face. **I will be as my own prophet and though all may laugh at my utterances they will hear my plans, they will know my dreams; and thus there will be no escape for me until my words become accomplished deeds.**

Today I will multiply my value a hundredfold.

I will commit not the terrible crime of aiming too low.

I will do the work that a failure will not do.

I will always let my reach exceed my grasp.

I will never be content with my performance in the market. I will always raise my goals as soon as they are attained.

I will always strive to make the next hour better than this one.

I will always announce my goals to the world.

Yet, never will I proclaim my accomplishments. Let the world, instead, approach me with praise and may I have the wisdom to receive it in humility.

Today I will multiply my value a hundredfold. One grain of wheat when multiplied a hundredfold will produce a hundred stalks. Multiply these a hundredfold, ten times, and they will feed all the cities of the earth. **Am I not more than a grain of wheat?** Today I will multiply my value a hundredfold. And when it is done I will do it again, and again, and there will be astonishment and wonder at my greatness as the words of these scrolls are fulfilled in me.

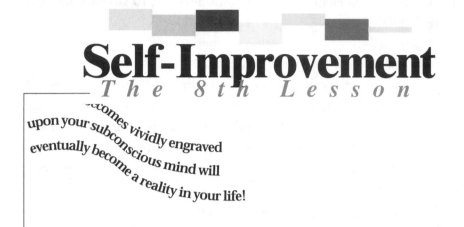

Self-Improvement
The 8th Lesson

...*comes* vividly engraved
upon your subconscious mind will
eventually become a reality in your life!

Now we come to the most pivotal point of this sales training program. During the introduction to these lessons, I mentioned that in order for a sales training program to be effective, it should increase sales profits. The principle contained in this eighth scroll is more directly related to increasing profits than any of the other nine scrolls. Within the context of this lesson you shall discover exactly how you can increase your sales profits and your personal income.

Out of all the strategies devised on how to multiply your value, only one can be applied by anyone at anytime and is the only one guaranteed not to fail. This mysterious principle is the Law of Increasing Returns. Because of its simple nature, the principle is often overlooked by those who believe that achieving success is a complicated undertaking. Yet, as you will see, it can easily be applied to increase your income and enhance every other area of your life.

1 | Value Multiplied by Genius
"A mulberry leaf touched with the genius of man becomes silk."

Whether you believe it or not, you are a genius. But you will never learn to develop and control your genius unless you believe you possess it. Every day more than 2,000 ideas pass through your mind and each time you act upon an idea you are exercising your powers of genius. Every action produces a reaction and these reactions eventually produce results. In other words, by acting upon ideas, you produce or create results in your life.

Using your creative genius without understanding how the process works is like walking around in the dark and bumping into things. You are constantly making things happen but you cannot see what they are or how they occur. In this chapter you'll discover how to use your creative powers to produce the results that you desire.

2 | The Multipliable Potential in Mankind
"I am likened to a grain of wheat..."

Mankind is a part of nature and is therefore subject to all natural laws. We have the ability to activate some natural laws, which operate instinctively in the plant and animal kingdom, through the power of choice. For instance, plants and animals instinctively reproduce, but mankind can either reproduce or refrain from reproducing — it is a matter of choice.

This brings us to the Law of Increasing Returns, a basic law of nature and the central focus of this chapter. In nature every seed sown produces a multiple harvest. The more seeds sown, the more abundant is the harvest. Therefore, the Law of Increasing Returns demands that every effort we exert produce a return of compensation. And to increase our returns, we need only to increase our efforts. Because it is so simple, this law is often overlooked.

Most people perform only the work for which they are paid. Although they want to be paid more, they wait until the opportunity to earn more presents itself. They look for this opportunity to come in the form of a better job or a promotion. They believe that when the chance to earn more comes they will do more.

The Law of Increasing Returns works in the opposite way. This law demands that when you do more than what you are paid to do, then you will be paid more.

3 | Increase Income by Enhancing Output
"Today I will multiply my value a hundredfold."

Whenever I challenge people to increase their efforts, I often hear the following pessimistic responses: "There is only so much I can do" or "There are only so many hours in a day." In anticipation of these doubts, I will reveal two ways to enhance your output regardless of what your present obligations may be.

Increasing output does not always mean increasing the quantity of work you do. You can also increase output by enhancing the quality. When you increase the quality of your product or service, you can charge more for it. When you increase the quality of follow-up on your customers and prospects, you can obtain more referrals. If you increase the quality of the process you use to conduct your business, you can get more work done in less time. Enhancing the process can give you the ability to increase your quantity because it will add hours to your day and power to your performance.

Another way to increase output is to increase the quantity of products sold or services rendered. You can decrease the time you spend closing a sale and increase the number of sales you close simply by taking greater advantage of today's technology. Computer software, fax machines, internet and e-mail, are all silent slaves waiting patiently to serve the sales master who will take the time to learn to use them more effectively.

4 | Nurturing Body and Mind

"Like the wheat grain which will sprout and blossom only if it is nurtured with rain and sun and warm winds, I too must nurture my body and mind to fulfill my dreams."

Some people seek financial success so they can just sit back and do nothing. That is not success; that's suicide. The moment anything ceases to grow, it begins to die. Since the same natural laws that govern all creation effect the growth of human life, it should be clear that the perpetual nurturing of body and mind are an indispensable part of our continued development. Failure to take care of your body will limit your ability to strive toward your goals because sales can be physically taxing. Therefore, nurture your body with healthy foods and exercise to help you reach your maximum potential.

The mind's consumption of knowledge is critical to our social and economic movement. To enhance your mental strength, simply develop an information diet that is more focused on your particular profession. Develop an insatiable appetite for books, tapes, videos, magazines, etc., which will aid you in achieving your dreams.

You should also increase your knowledge in areas that may not be directly related to your business. Reading books on health, finances, relationships and other areas of life can empower you with insight to better manage those areas and free your mind to think more clearly so that you can more effectively pursue your goals.

5 | The Power and Process of Goal Setting

"First I will set goals for the day, the week, the year and my life."

Goal setting is the most powerful personal achievement tool. Most people have general goals; you need to make them clear with specific steps and time limits for achieving them. Otherwise, you will not complete them all. Goal setting is like creating your own rungs on your ladder to success. If you just keep making the rungs and continue to climb them one after another, you can eventually climb to any level of success that you desire.

6 | Setting Yourself Up For a Fall
"The height of my goals will not hold me in awe though I may stumble often before they are reached."

After reaching for a goal and failing to achieve it, most people become fearful of trying again. It is like being thrown from a horse; unless you get back on you will never learn to ride. Don't let the fear of falling cause you to become paralyzed in mediocrity. The best way to avoid this is to realize that every time you set too high a goal, you are setting yourself up for a fall.

Each time you set a goal that would elevate you to a higher level of achievement, it requires you to stretch yourself, to expand your capacity to perform. In reaching for that next level, chances are that you may stumble and fall at the beginning. But if you keep trying you will soon master that level and prepare to move on to the next.

If you recognize that falling (mistakes and temporary setbacks) is simply a part of the process, you will not easily become discouraged and quit. Perhaps you may need to take smaller steps in order to reach your goal, but you don't have to make your goals smaller simply because you're afraid of falling. Falling along the way to success is not equal to failing, unless you don't pick yourself up and try again.

7 | Surpass Your Own Achievements

"To surpass the deeds of others is unimportant; to surpass my own deeds is all."

Striving competitively to outdo others can sometimes be hazardous to your own progress. Some people look at the accomplishments of great achievers and think, "One day I will beat them because I am better than they are." Doing this is destructive because it causes you to seek your value through a false sense of superiority to others. Such an attitude creates envy, resentment and hostility. Even if you surpass someone's achievements, you will throw other areas of your life out of balance and end up with an empty victory.

Striving to outdo others also causes you to lose perspective on your progress. We see the results achievers produce, but we have no idea of the amount of time and effort they invested to produce those results.

The safest and most effective way to insure your own progress is to use your past achievements as the starting point. If your present performance is just one percent better than your past performance, then you are clearly making progress. Striving to surpass your own achievements enables you to keep sight of your progress while developing an attitude of self-satisfaction, self-confidence and high self-esteem. This allows you to savor the sweet taste of your own personal victories.

8 | Use the Gift of Prophecy

"I will be my own prophet and though all may laugh at my utterances they will hear my plans, they will know my dreams; and thus there will be no escape for me until my words become accomplished deeds."

Prophecy is a statement about what will happen in the future. It is more than a mere prediction of what you think may happen; it is a declaration of what you know will happen. You might ask, "How can I make a prophecy when I don't know what will happen in the future?" You should know that you make a prophecy almost every day. Every promise you make is a prophecy, if you really intend to keep it.

Don't be afraid to declare what you want for your future. If you only declare it to yourself, the simple act of declaring it will help motivate you. However, when you make your declaration to others, you have a greater accountability, a positive peer pressure that causes you to strive harder to make the prophecy come true. Identify a single goal that you can declare today as a statement of prophecy, announce it to the world and watch it ignite the fires of your determination to follow through.

9 | The Crime of Mediocrity
"I will commit not the terrible crime of aiming too low."

While robbery is an obvious crime, the crime of trading your tremendous talents and potential for a life of mediocrity is not. Although robbery is often considered the more serious of the two, people who sell themselves short rob the world of a great blessing that could enrich humanity. They rob their family and friends of the many benefits they could all enjoy, and they rob themselves of the fulfillment and satisfaction that their life was designed to produce.

Aiming too low is not a crime punishable by our judicial system; it is punishable by the universal laws that govern life.

10 | Comparing Humans to Plants
"Am I not more than a grain of wheat?"

If plant life has the ability to multiply its value, then surely humans should be able to multiply their value as well. Many interesting parallels exist between plants and humans. However, unlike plants, humans have the power to choose whether they multiply in value or simply wither and die. The power of choice gives you an advantage over plant life, for you have the ability to multiply your value at will.

In his classic book *As a Man Thinketh,* James Allen reveals how humans can determine the fruit they will harvest in life by controlling the thoughts they allow to take root in their minds. He also explains that if we fail to control the thoughts growing in our minds, our lives will only produce a harvest of useless weeds. By dealing effectively with the root cause of thoughts that produce the harvest in your life you can keep many undesirable weeds from sprouting up in the first place.

The ideas contained in this chapter should provide you with sufficient insight into how you can multiply your value and increase your income. Now all you have to do is begin planting the seeds by giving that extra effort. Don't wait for the opportunity; create the opportunity. The world around you is just like a fertile field. If you plant good things in it, it will yield a harvest of good things. Likewise, if you plant negative things, you will only reap a harvest of weeds and thorns. Should you desire to change the harvest you have been reaping, you can easily do so by simply changing the types of seeds you plant.

❗ Developing Progress:
A Practical Exercise

In order for a sales training program to be effective it should ultimately increase sales profits. But even if you possessed the answers to all of life's great mysteries, they would be of no value, unless you put them to use. If you do the following exercise, you will increase your profits.

Ideas are the source of all value. An idea acted upon is equal to a financial transaction. Look around you. There is nothing in the world that we spend money for that did not originate from an idea. Bill Gates, one of the wealthiest people in the world, obtained his wealth from selling ideas, packaged in the form of software. Although ideas don't begin as visible material things, you should always realize the value they hold.

Some people go to great lengths to find a coin they dropped from their pocket or to pick up a coin that they find lying on the sidewalk. When valuable ideas drop from your mind, or when you stumble upon brilliant ideas, you should treat them as if they are cold hard cash because IDEAS ARE MONEY!

Think about that statement until it has penetrated your consciousness and you believe it. And consider this: money is merely a medium of exchange. This means that the value of money lies in what it can be exchanged for. Likewise, ideas are a medium of exchange because the value of an idea also lies in what it can be exchanged for.

You might want to create an idea bank where you can store your ever-multiplying value. Use a notebook that is devoted exclusively to ideas. Develop the habit of regularly recording the best ideas that cross your mind each day. Each week, review these ideas and deposit the best one on a special page within your idea bank. Once a month, review the most outstanding weekly ideas and select the best idea for that month. This process will yield you no less than 12 premium ideas over the course of each year.

Here are a few other sources for ideas you can deposit within your bank:

1. Create a suggestion box where people can submit ideas privately.
2. Put up a bulletin board in your home or office where people can post ideas openly.
3. Host a brainstorming session where ideas can be generated around a single topic.
4. Offer rewards for good ideas submitted to address a particular problem.
5. Collect ideas from your friends, family, and even customers.
6. Keep a note pad by your bed to catch the ideas that come when you're nearly asleep.

Take the best ideas and put them to work; take the others and put them in safe keeping. Some of the ideas you have no use for now could prove to be of tremendous value to you in the future.

Spotlight on:
Anthony Robbins

At the age of nineteen Anthony Robbins had achieved a degree of success that many never do. Generating $5,000 to $10,000 a month in personal income, he had become known as the "Wonder Boy" of his industry.

After sabotaging his own success by neglecting to consistently act on the success principles he had learned, he found himself 38 pounds overweight, depressed and totally broke financially, emotionally and spiritually. Finally he recommitted himself to discovering the key to producing lasting success. In examining the lives of successful people Anthony found Personal Power (which is the ability to consistently take action toward your goals) to be the missing key. Since making this discovery Anthony Robbins has applied his own personal power to achieve amazingly successful results. He is the nation's foremost authority on the psychology of peak performance and personal, professional, and organizational turnaround—an identity he has established through his ability to consistently help individuals and organizations create measurable results over the last 20 years. In 1997 he was honored as one of the ten "Outstanding People of the World" by the International Chamber of Commerce, and has been called one of the great influencers

138 |

of this generation.

Achievers who have already reached the pinnacle of success call on Anthony Robbins to take their lives to the next level. Mr. Robbins has advised and counseled Fortune 500 CEOs, members of two royal families, sports teams from the NHL and NBA, professional athletes ranging from Andre Agassi to Greg Norman, outstanding students, extraordinary parents, and the president of the United States.

Because of his ability to develop systems for creating immediate change in virtually any situation—regardless of how daunting the circumstances—Anthony Robbins is also sought after by those seriously challenged by life: individuals facing depression, frustration, loneliness, or challenges in their relationships, finances, physical health, or life management skills.

Anthony Robbins is a best-selling author, and his educational audio system, Personal Power, is the number one personal and professional development system of all time—more than 30 million tapes are being used to transform lives worldwide. He has addressed distinguished audiences from Britain's Parliament to the Harvard Business School.

For two decades, Anthony Robbins has devoted his life to providing critical resources of caring, education, and inspiration, as well as specific strategies and tools for helping those most in need: the homeless, the elderly, prisoners, and inner-city youngsters. He provides numerous scholarships, products and programs to non-profit organizations internationally. In the last few years alone, his non-profit Anthony Robbins Foundation has fed more than a quarter-million people in over 200 cities worldwide.

❗ Discovering the Secrets
• of the Successful ▪▬▬ ▬

How did you get started in the field of sales?

[compiled by the editorial staff] In 1978, at 18 years old, Tony found a job that advertised "Make $500 a week as a manager in training—no experience necessary." Tony assumed he was management material, so he applied to the Pearl Music Company, which turned out to be a door-to-door job selling Pearl's music club.

One night, while he was selling the music club at a man's house, the man started telling Tony that he was the greatest persuader he had ever seen in his life - and that he should take his skills and use them to change people's lives. Tony replied, "Well, that's actually my long-term goal." So the man told Tony there was a great speaker and role model Tony should meet—a man named Jim Rohn. Tony couldn't believe his ears. He had already been to Rohn's seminar and wanted to work for him. This man claimed to be a good friend of Rohn, and invited Tony to attend a seminar as his guest.

A few weeks later, Tony arrived at the South Coast Plaza Hotel to attend Rohn's seminar, only to discover that no one knew the man who had offered Tony the ticket. Finally, one person said, "Hey, I know who you're talking about, but that guy definitely doesn't know Jim Rohn!" Nevertheless, they let a thrilled Tony sit in on the seminar anyway. Tony, who had been to Rohn's seminars before, knew the material backward and forward, and sat in his chair finishing Rohn's sentences before the lecturer did. During the break, Tony approached Rohn and said that he wanted to work for him. Rohn told Tony, "Young man, you can do that. All you have to do is invest in all our products." The cost was $1,200, which Tony didn't have.

Believing that people always get what they must have, Tony went to every bank he could find looking for a loan. Finally, he convinced a woman at the Bank of America in West Covina to give it to him. Tony bought Rohn's products and got the job.

Unfortunately, the Pearl Music Company did not want Tony to have two jobs. Neither were they pleased that Tony was selling the Jim Rohn seminar to his music customers.

Tony continued to persevere, however, and as he began to succeed earning $3,000 his first month with Jim Rohn. Tony then went back for a final assembly at his old school, arriving in style and feeling very proud. People were worried about him, but he told them not to. He was doing what he loved, he was helping people, and he was making $3,000 a month doing it.

What is the greatest challenge you have had to face over the years?
No matter how prepared you are, there's one thing that I can absolutely guarantee: if you're on the river of life, it's likely you're going to hit a few rocks. That's not being negative; that's being accurate. The key is that when you do run aground, instead of beating yourself up for being such a "failure," remember that there are no failures in life. There are only results. If you didn't get the results you wanted, learn from this experience so that you have references about how to make better decisions in the future. So many people want to avoid any hint of a problem or challenge, yet surmounting difficulty is the crucible that forms character.

Having said that, I have had many character building experiences in my life. For example, at one point, I discovered that someone in our company had embezzled funds, leaving us $756,000 in debt. Rather than focus on the problem, I focused on now to create long-term solutions—not simply for that event alone, but for creating systems to ensure that this could never happen again. Experts were advising me to declare bankruptcy—but I refused to even consider that as an option. Since that time, my company has achieved record breaking profits every year—and this last year we were able to distribute US $300,000 cash in bonuses to our employees.

Every time I am faced with a challenge, I ask myself a series of questions:
1. What can I learn from this?
2. What's great about this, or what could be great about this?

3. What's not perfect yet?

4. What am I willing to do to make it the way I want it?

5. What am I willing to not do to make it the way I want it?

6. How can I enjoy doing the things necessary to make it the way I want it?

What do you consider to be the most outstanding achievement of your career?

Success to me is the ongoing process of striving to become more. It is the opportunity to continually grow emotionally, socially, spiritually, physiologically and intellectually, while contributing in some positive way to others.

My life has always been about helping people create an extraordinary quality of life—and now my challenge is to find the best vehicle for reaching the largest number of people in the most empowering way. So many opportunities have presented themselves to me, and I'm thrilled with the possibilities. For example, I'm a member of the Advisory Board of the United Nations Health and Science Council, which has given me a unique platform—and new thoughts about how I can best help individuals, organizations and even nations in the new millennium. The bottom line is that people have within them a force that is so powerful that once they unleash or tap into it, there is nothing that can keep them from doing, being, sharing, creating and giving whatever they envision in life. My life is committed to helping them to unleash that power, and to create the extraordinary quality of life they desire and deserve.

Who were some of you most influential role models and mentors?

There have been many outstanding people who have touched my life in so many ways. A few who stand out, however, are:

1. Jim Rohn, who was my very first teacher. He taught me that it's not what you get in this life but who you become in the process that is most important.

2. Richard Bandler and John Grinder, who are the founders of NLP (Neuro Linguistic Programming). They taught me not only that rapid change is possible, but many of the specific tools and strategies to create change and make it last.

3. Becky's father, Cecil Biggerstaff. This gentle soul knew that it's the littlest things in life that make the biggest difference. Our lives are made up of moments. If you don't capture and notice them, life passes you by.

4. My wife Becky and my children, Tyler, Jolie, Josh, and Jairek. My family is my greatest joy and passion in life—their constant examples of unconditional love and joy continually astound me. I learn from them constantly and am truly blessed to have such incredible, talented caring people around me.

I have many favorite quotes from many spectacular people throughout history. Just one of my favorites is by Nelson Mandela:

> "Our deepest fear is not that we are inadequate.
> Our deepest fear is that we are powerful beyond measure.
> It is our light, not our darkness, that most frightens us.
> We ask ourselves, who am I to be brilliant, gorgeous, talented, and fabulous?
> Actually, who are you not to be? You are a child of God.
> Your playing small doesn't serve the world.
> There's nothing enlightened about shrinking so that other people won't feel insecure around you.
> We were born to make manifest the glory of God that is within us.
> It's not just in some of us; it's in everyone.
> And as we let our own light shine, we unconsciously give other people permission to do the same.
> As we are liberated from our own fear, our presence automatically liberates others."

What is the most valuable advice you can offer an aspiring sales person?

Successful individuals have a unique ability to focus in ways which allow them to persist until they make the distinctions that put them over the top. In every walk of life, those who succeed know the power of continuously pursuing their vision, even if all the details of how to achieve it are not yet apparent. Success is not an accident. There are consistent, logical patterns of action, specific pathways to excellence, that are within the reach of us all. Those individuals who achieve extraordinary success share a commitment to taking action. But what is it that gets them to continue day after day to put everything they've got in to everything they do?

There are character traits that successful—and more importantly, fulfilled—people cultivate within themselves. Each person must individually determine these characteristics, what I call power virtues, and draw upon them consistently in order to create an extraordinary quality of life. Several of the power virtues that I consider to be most important and that I draw upon consistently in my own life are: determination, faith, compassion, courage, and of course, passion. Passion gives life power and juice and meaning. There is no greatness without a passion to be great, whether it's the aspiration of an athlete or an artist, a scientist, a parent, or a businessman. Passion can turn any challenge into a tremendous opportunity. Passion is unbridled power to move our lives forward at a faster tempo than ever before.

Ten Ancient Scrolls

Anthony Robbins

O g Mandino was a master of inspiration and motivation. His writings have impacted the lives of millions in a very positive way. The ten ancient scrolls from *The Greatest Salesman in the World* are without question the most profound description ever given on the qualities required to achieve success in sales and life.

The **9**th**Action**
Scroll

My dreams are worthless, my plans are dust, my goals are impossible.

All are of no value unless they are followed by action.

I will act now. Never has there been a map, however carefully executed to detail and scale, which carried its owner over even one inch of ground. Never has there been a parchment of law, however fair, which prevented one crime. Never has there been a scroll, even such as the one I hold, which earned so much as a penny or produced a single word of acclamation. Action, alone, is the tinder which ignites the map, the parchment, this scroll, my dreams, my plans, my goals, into a living force. **Action is the food and drink, which will nourish my success.**

I will act now. **My procrastination which has held me back was born of fear** and now I recognize this secret mined from the depths of all courageous hearts. **Now I know that to conquer fear I must always act without hesitation and the flutters in my heart will**

vanish. Now I know that action reduces the lion of terror to an ant of equanimity.

I will act now. Henceforth, I will remember the lesson of the firefly that gives of its light only when it is on the wing, only when it is in action. I will become a firefly and even in the day my glow will be seen in spite of the sun. Let others be as butterflies that preen their wings yet depend on the charity of a flower for life. I will be as the firefly and my light will brighten the world.

I will act now.

I will not avoid the tasks of today and charge them to tomorrow for I know that tomorrow never comes. Let me act now even though my actions may not bring happiness or success for it is better to act and fail than not to act and flounder. Happiness, in truth, may not be the fruit plucked by my action yet without action all fruit will die on the vine.

I will act now.

I will act now. I will act now. **I will act now. Henceforth, I will repeat these words again and again and again, each hour, each day, every day, until the words become as much a habit as my breathing and the actions which follow become as instinctive as the blinking of my eyelids. With these words I can condition my mind to perform every act necessary for my success.** With these words I can condition my mind to meet every challenge which the failure avoids.

I will act now.

I will repeat these words again and again and again.

When I awake I will say them and leap from my cot while the failure sleeps yet another hour.

I will act now.

When I enter the market place I will say them and immediately confront my first prospect while the failure ponders yet his possibility of rebuff.

I will act now.

When I face a closed door I will say them and knock while the failure waits outside with fear and trepidation.

I will act now.

When I face temptation I will say them and immediately act to remove myself from evil. I will act now. When I am tempted to quit and begin again tomorrow I will say them and immediately act to consummate another sale.

I will act now. **Only action determines my value in the market place and to multiply my value I will multiply my actions.** I will walk where the failure fears to walk. I will work when the failure seeks rest. I will talk when the failure remains silent. I will call on ten who can buy my goods while the failure makes grand plans to call on one. I will say it is done before the failure says it is too late.

I will act now.

For now is all I have. Tomorrow is the day reserved for the labor of the lazy. I am not lazy. Tomorrow is the day when the evil become good. I am not evil. Tomorrow is the day when the weak become strong. I am not weak. Tomorrow is the day when the failure will succeed. I am not a failure.

I will act now.

When the lion is hungry he eats. When the eagle has thirst he drinks. Lest they act, both will perish.

I hunger for success. I thirst for happiness and peace of mind. Lest I act I will perish in a life of failure, misery, and sleepless nights.

I will command, and I will obey mine own command.

I will act now.

Success will not wait. If I delay she will become betrothed to another and lost to me forever.

This is the time. This is the place. I am the man.

I will act now.

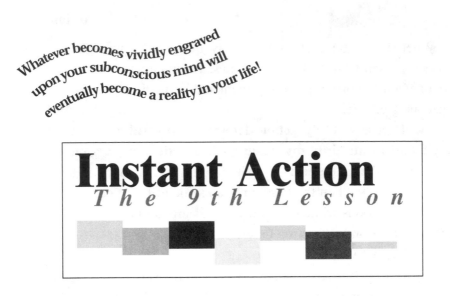

Whatever becomes vividly engraved upon your subconscious mind will eventually become a reality in your life!

Instant Action
T h e 9 t h L e s s o n

You already know a number of things you need to do in order to become a successful salesperson. Some of these things you may have known long before you began reading this book. Nevertheless, you must admit to yourself that there are several things you know you should do that you still have not done. Why? Could it be the persistent "P" word?

Procrastination is a common trait, so rest assured you are not alone. However, one of the major differences between a successful person and a failure is that the successful person will consistently perform in a much different way. What makes extraordinary people extraordinary is that they do the little EXTRA things which ORDINARY people neglect.

America's free enterprise system is specifically designed to reward those who take action without being told to do so. Therefore, pay close attention to the ninth scroll. It will strengthen your initiative and show you how to break the paralyzing habit of procrastination by helping you to better understand its cause and its cure.

1 | The Lifeless Nature of Dreams

"My dreams are worthless, my plans are dust, my goals are impossible. All are of no value unless they are followed by action."

A dream is nothing more than a wish or a fantasy. However, you can choose to yield your body, mind and soul to your dream, and thus give it a life of its own. When you live your life for the fulfillment of your dream, it is as if you have become possessed by some enchanting spirit. Every action you take transports another segment of the dream into reality.

In this same manner, our nightmares can also become realities when we give in to our greatest fears. But whether it is your fondest dream or your most dreadful nightmare, you alone determine which will have life through the actions you choose.

2 | Action is the Fuel of Success

"Action is the food and drink, which will nourish my success."

You already possess the raw material necessary to produce success. Your dream is the seed and your ability to take action is the nourishment needed to cause your seed to bear fruit, although activity does not always equal productivity.

Often people busy themselves with activity in order to keep their minds off the unfulfilling aspects of their lives. To them activity is like a drug, which they use to escape reality. They hide behind it like a facade so that the rest of the world will think they are happily engaged in an important task.

Your life is a field of unlimited possibilities; if you focus your activities on cultivating success, success will flourish. If you want to succeed in any area of your life, you must nourish that area daily through your actions. If there are some undesirable things growing in your life, then simply cut them off at the source. Stop feeding and nourishing them and watch them eventually whither and die. The bounty of success is within your grasp, you need only to reach out and take it.

3 | Cause of Procrastination
"My procrastination, which has held me back, was born of fear."

One of the reasons we put things off is because we are afraid they may produce undesirable results. Your fear could be based on any number of things or even a combination of things. Only you can determine the source of your fear. Yet, even more important than identifying the source of your fear, is your need to understand the substance from which fear is made. Fear is fashioned from mental images of what might happen.

The better you understand the nature of fear, the easier it becomes to examine the fears that cause your procrastination. Fear is sometimes nothing more than an image, a picture in your mind of some undesirable event. To neutralize the fear you simply need to change the images that dominate your thinking.

4 | Conquering the Butterflies
"Now I know that to conquer fear I must always act without hesitation and the flutters in my heart will vanish."

You have the ability to change the sensation you feel from fear's image simply by making a slight change in the image. Imagine that a strong wind is blowing in your face. You can feel the wind in your hair, on your cheeks and even rustling in your clothes. The wind becomes so strong that it causes your eyes to squint and makes it difficult for you to catch your breath. Now, to stop the discomfort, simply turn around with your back to the wind. Although the wind is still blowing, by turning around you begin to experience a more positive sensation.

Likewise, you can change the sensation you experience from an image simply by turning the image around in your mind. It requires no more imagination to visualize a positive outcome than it does to visualize a negative one. Neither of the images is real, but the one you visualize has a greater chance of becoming a reality. To conquer fear the first action you should take is to turn your negative image into a positive one. Once you create a positive image you can take the action needed to make it a reality.

5 | The Taming of Fear
"**Now I know that action reduces the lion of terror into an ant of equanimity.**"

One of the most effective ways to stop fears from running wild in your mind is to take some direct physical action to counteract them. Fear takes a molehill and turns it into a mountain, but action brings it back to the original size.

Take a moment and think of one area where fear is present in your life. Perhaps it is in business, a relationship, or maybe a health condition. Now imagine one action you could take that would lessen the intensity of your fear. Often taking that action is all that's needed to send fear running away.

6 The Myth of Tomorrow

"I will not avoid the task of today and charge them to tomorrow for I know that tomorrow never comes."

Often a parent attempts to deceive his child with a promise of tomorrow, which he has no intention of keeping. "Tomorrow," he says, "tomorrow, I promise." All along the parent knows that the only reason he made the promise was to escape the responsibility of having to do something TODAY. He naively thinks that the child will buy the lie, and by tomorrow, will have forgotten all about it. Thus, the parent will have successfully dodged an obligation once again.

However, the child does not forget so easily and will only tolerate broken promises for so long. If the pattern continues, the child will eventually lose all confidence in anything the parent says. In this same manner, the empty commitments we sometimes make to escape the responsibilities of today often cause us to lose confidence in ourselves.

Don't postpone important tasks until some imaginary point in time. Do those tasks now, for today is the only day to which you have access.

7 Developing the Action Habit

"I will act now ... I will repeat these words ... until the words become as much a habit as my breathing and the actions which follow become as instinctive as the blinking of my eyelids."

To move a part of the body, the brain must send an electrical impulse to the particular muscle where the impulse triggers the desired reaction in the body. With children and adults, the process seems instantaneous, as if it required no thought at all. However, observe how much effort infants put into this process. They concentrate intensely and struggle just to reach out for a toy, or maneuver their bottles to their mouths. Then, after months of practice, what was once a challenge, becomes second nature.

So it is with the development of the action habit. You must send the message to your subconscious by repeating your commitment to act now. After practicing this for some time you will soon develop a degree of spontaneity you may have never thought you could achieve.

Every time you are tempted to postpone or delay a task, simply repeat the words aloud, "I will act now!" Don't analyze whether the task is worthy of being delayed, and don't concern yourself with whether or not you actually follow through. Just repeat the words, "I will act now!" and you will soon develop the urge to follow through. Eventually, like the infant, your practice of this process will make what was once a major challenge seem like second nature.

8 | Conditioning the Mind for Success
"With these words I can condition my mind to perform every act necessary for my success."

Investing time and energy to condition the human machine is a wise thing to do. Some people will go to great lengths to condition every other part of their human machine, yet they neglect to condition its most important component, the mind.

Although you might say, "I do condition my mind with education, reading and even an occasional crossword puzzle." That is not the conditioning I am talking about. That type of conditioning refers to developing a standardized reflex or behavior pattern in response to various types of stimulus. The "act now reflex" is the conditioning you need to achieve success.

The simple act of repeating the words over and over again will not make you successful. Yet, repeating the words will cause the idea to become a part of your subconscious attitude and gradually condition the pattern of behavior that will create success.

9 | Your Actions Determine Your Value

"Only action determines my value in the marketplace and to multiply my value I will multiply my actions."

Your net worth does not determine your value to the world around you. To your customers and prospects in the marketplace, the value you hold is determined by the degree of benefit you bring to their lives. A glass of cold water has absolutely no value to a thirsty man unless he can drink it. Likewise, although you may possess tremendous potential, unless you develop your potential so that it benefits others, it is worthless in the marketplace.

We do not increase our value by increasing the volume of what we get, but rather by increasing the volume of what we give.

Every act is a seed that will create the plant of a corresponding reaction, and eventually produce the fruitful harvest of an ultimate result. If you desire a more abundant harvest, then you need to increase the number of action seeds you sow.

10 | Hunger Motivates You to Take Action

"I hunger for success. I thirst for happiness and peace of mind."

I once heard a minister tell a story about a young Native American boy's desire to become successful. He sought advice from some of the wisest people in his community. "You should go and talk with the old sage who lives beyond the forest high up in the mountains," they told him. So the young boy set off and journeyed for days until he finally came upon an old man, rocking contentedly on the front porch of his huge and luxurious mansion. "I have come to discover the pathway to success, for I was told that you can show me," he said to the old man. Without a sound or expression, the old man rose from his rocker and slowly walked passed the boy and down the hill to the edge of a flowing stream. The boy watched the old man as he walked knee deep, waist deep, and then chest deep into the water. Raising his hands the old man beckoned the boy to follow him into the water.

As the boy approached, the old man placed his hands behind the boy's neck and lowered the lad's head beneath the water. After a few seconds the boy attempted to lift his head but the old man firmly held it under the water. Once the youth began to struggle violently to breathe the old man released him. The boy broke for the shore and as soon as he caught his breath he shouted, "Are you crazy, old man? I thought you were going to show me the way to success." As he emerged from the water the old man calmly replied, "When you want success as badly as you wanted to breathe, THEN it will be yours."

Developing Action: A Practical Exercise

The following exercise is designed to help you strengthen your action muscles. Since we know that all action does not always equal productivity, let's focus on some specific areas. The following are areas where the action you take can produce corresponding profits. For each of the tasks, make a commitment to do the following three things:

1. Set aside a specific time you will regularly devote to this particular task.
2. Set a measurable goal for the results you intend to produce.
3. Keep a written record of the results you create and strive to improve on your record.

Making calls — Know what you want to say and the results you seek before you call.

Seeing contacts — Try to pre-schedule a number of contacts within the same area.

Sending correspondence — Use form letters and database merging whenever possible.

Closing sales — Decrease the close time for each sale and increase the number of closes.

Requesting referrals — Make getting referrals a part of your close and follow up process.

Doing the follow up — Create a follow-up system that creates repeat and referral business.

The following are eight areas where taking the proper action will produce increased bottom line profits. Use your creativity to determine a course of action that would be proper for your particular situation.

Cutting expenses — Devise a way to reduce the cost of closing each sale.

Reducing turnaround time — Cut delivery time without cutting the value of your product or service.

Increasing customers — Expand your territory or enhance your penetration.

Increasing amount of initial purchase — Sell more initial units by creating packaged deals.

Increasing the price for items — Enhancing perceived value could yield large returns.

Distributing coupon — Give prospects a value that they will lose unless they buy something.

Running a special — Give a boost to slow moving products or services.

Building a network — Trade off leads with others in related or unrelated industries.

In Brian Tracy's series *The Psychology of Selling* he offers a powerful suggestion for increasing personal productivity. It is to write out a number of ideas that you can use to resolve a problem or address an issue that you are dealing with. Mr. Tracy suggests that you write out a total of 20 ideas on a standard sheet of notebook paper. Use this process to stretch your thinking and prepare you for the final phase of this exercise.

   Write out 20 actions that you can take to increase your sales profits or personal income. You may use some of the ideas that appear here if you wish. When you have completed your list write one action you will take within the following time frames. Make the level of difficulty appropriate for the time allotted.

One action you will take today.

_____

One action you will take this week.

_____

One action you will take this month.

_____

One action you will take this year.

_____

Brian Tracy
Author • Speaker • Consultant

*B*rian Tracy was born in Canada but raised in Pomona, California. At the age of sixteen he dropped out of school and earned money washing dishes and working in factories and construction. At the age of twenty-one Brian packed up and drove across county in an old car. A few years later he went off to see the world and didn't return for ten years. While out exploring, he made his way to Africa, and it was there that he experienced an incident that made an incredible impact on his life. In 1965 his Land Rover broke down midway across the Sahara Desert. He knew that if he and his friends couldn't fix the car they would die. It was then that something locked in and he realized he was responsible for his own life. Needless to say they managed to fix the car and escape death in the desert, but the experience, he says, taught him this valuable lesson. "You must be clear about the goals you set, flexible about the process of achieving them, and then continually learn all you can in every way possible."

Today Brian Tracy is one of America's leading authorities on the development of human potential and personal effectiveness. He's a dynamic and entertaining speaker with a wonderful ability to inform

and inspire audiences toward peak performance and high levels of achievement. He addresses thousands of men and women each year on the subjects of personal and professional development, including the executives and staff of IBM, Arthur Andersen, McDonnell Douglas and The Million-Dollar Round Table. His exciting talks and seminars on leadership, self-esteem, goals and strategy, creativity and success psychology bring about immediate changes and long-term results. Brian has a B.A. in Communications and an M.A., and is the Chairman of Brian Tracy International, a human resource company based in San Diego, California, with affiliates throughout America and in 31 countries worldwide.

Prior to founding Brian Tracy International, Brian was the chief operating officer of a development company with $265 million in assets and $75 million in annual sales. He has had successful careers in sales and marketing, investments, real estate development and syndication, importation, distribution, and management consulting. He has conducted high-level consulting assignments with several billion-dollar-plus corporations in strategic planning and organizational devel-opment.

He is the author/narrator of best-selling audio-cassette programs, including: *The Psychology of Achievement, Fast Track to Business Success, The Psychology of Selling, Peak Performance Woman, The Psychology of Success,* and *24 Techniques for Closing the Sale.* Brian is also the author of *Maximum Achievement* and *Advanced Selling Strategies.*

! • | Discovering the Secrets of the Successful

How did you get started in the field of sales?
At the age of 10, I began selling soap, door-to-door, to earn my way to summer camp. Later I sold newspapers and then lawn mowing services. As my career evolved, I sold office supplies from office to office. I sold mutual funds and other investments from business to business. Over time, I have sold advertising, automobiles, real estate, investments, training and consulting services, and a variety of other things.

What is the greatest challenge you have had to face over the years?
In my experience, life is a continuous succession of problems and difficulties, only broken by the occasional crisis. Over the years, the greatest challenge has always been to be absolutely clear about my goals, and then to persist through every adversity until those goals have been achieved. This is an ongoing challenge.

What do you consider to be the most outstanding achievement of your career?
My working career to date covers 35 years, 80 countries, more than 22 different jobs and more challenges, changes, difficulties and opportunities that I can count or remember. Perhaps the achievement with which I am most happy is my decision to be a professional speaker and consultant and then to eventually achieve success in this field.

Who were some of you most influential role models and mentors?
My role models have been successful men and women throughout the ages, going back to the great leaders like Cyrus the Great of Persia, Hannibal of Carthage, and Alexander of Massedon. I have studied history and historical figures right up to the present day. My "mentors" in business today are people like Peter Drucker, Andrew Grove, Earl Nightinggale, Jim Rohn, and countless others who have made signifi-

cant contributions to individual and organizational effectiveness.

What is the most effective sales technique you have ever used?

I have written hundreds of pages, recorded dozens of hours on audio and video and trained more than one million salespeople worldwide. Perhaps the most effective technique I have discovered is the simple approach of establishing rapport by asking questions, taking time to uncover the clients true needs, and then presenting my product or service as the ideal solution to the customer problem. This simple approach embraces Relationship Selling, Consultative Selling, Strategic Selling, Educational Selling and virtually all other forms of selling that work in today's competitive marketplace.

Given an example of how you would apply this technique in a real life situation?

There is no mystery to this technique. Simply become more interested in helping the client than in selling your product or service. Ask questions. Listen attentively to the answers. Make suggestions and recommendations. Ask the client to make a decision. This works for virtually everyone always.

What is the most valuable advice you can offer to an aspiring salesperson?

The very best advice I could offer is for a salesperson to start off by selling something that he or she really likes, enjoys and wants to use and sell to his or her mother or father.

Then, become an absolute expert in that field. Learn everything there is to learn bout your product or service so that you can sell it anywhere, under any conditions, without any sales material or literature. The third thing I would recommend is that salespeople learn to persist until they eventually succeed. If they do persist, they will succeed.

If you have not always lived by your current philosophy, what provoked the change?

I have always lived by the philosophy that I both practice and preach. People who have known me for as long as 25 years will say that I have really never changed over the years. I have always been the same person both internally and externally.

On Og Mandino's
Ten Ancient Scrolls
Brian Tracy

O g Mandino was truly a literary genius because his books were written in such easy to understand terms. In fact, Og told me on occasion that the reason his books were so easy to read is because they were so hard to write. The ten ancient scrolls summarize the entire school of success and make the information more accessible to the reader.

Scholars and professors have written thousands of books on the subject of success, many of which are completely true, yet totally useless. If the reader has to wrestle with the information to understand what is written, it will be of little use because pcople need material that is relevant and immediately applicable. Og Mandino's scrolls are a helpful tool to the sales professional because they are easy to understand and help to modify behavior, as a result they enhance the salesperson's ability to achieve success.

The 10th Prayer
Scroll

Who is of so little faith that in a moment of great disaster or heartbreak has not called to his God? Who has not cited out when confronted with danger, death, or mystery beyond his normal experience or comprehension? **From where has this deep instinct come which escapes from the mouth of all living creatures in moments of peril?**

Move your hand in haste before another's eyes and his eyelids will blink. Tap another on his knee and his leg will jump. Confront another with dark horror and his mouth will say, "My God" from the same deep impulse.

My life need not be filled with religion in order for me to recognize this greatest mystery of nature. All creatures that walk the earth, including man, possess the instinct to cry for help. Why do we possess this instinct, this gift?

Are not our cries a form of prayer? Is it not incomprehensible in a world governed by nature's laws to give a lamb, or a mule, or a bird, or man the instinct to cry out for help lest some great mind has also provided that the cry should be heard by some superior power having the ability to hear and to answer our cry? **Henceforth I will pray,** but my cries for help will only be cries for guidance. Never will I pray for the material things of the world. I am not calling to a servant to bring me food. I am not ordering an innkeeper to provide me with room. Never will I seek delivery of gold, love, good health, petty victories, fame, success, or happiness. **Only for guidance will I pray, that I may be shown the way to acquire these things, and my prayer will always be answered.**

The guidance I seek may come, or the guidance I seek may not come, but are not both of these an answer? If a child seeks bread from his father and it is not forthcoming has not the father answered? I will pray for guidance, and I will pray as a salesman, in this manner:

Oh creator of all things, help me. For this day I go out into the world naked and alone, and without your hand to guide me I will wander far from the path which leads to success and happiness.

I ask not for gold or garments or even opportunities equal to my ability; instead, guide me so that I may acquire ability equal to my opportunities. You have taught the lion and the eagle how to hunt and prosper with teeth and claw. **Teach me how to hunt with words and prosper with love so that I may be a lion among men and an eagle in the market place.**

Help me to remain humble through obstacles and failures; *yet hide not from mine eyes the prize that will come with victory.*

Assign me tasks to which others have failed; yet guide me to pluck the seeds of success from their failures. Confront me with fears that will temper my spirit, yet endow me with courage to laugh at my misgivings.

Spare me sufficient days to reach my goals; yet help me to live this day as though it be my last.

Guide me in my words that they may bear fruit; yet silence me from gossip that none be maligned.

Discipline me in the habit of trying and trying again; yet show me the way to make use of the law of averages. **Favor me with alertness to recognize opportunity;** *yet endow me with patience that will concen-*

trate my strength. Bathe me in good habits that the bad ones may drown; yet grant me compassion for weaknesses in others. Suffer me to know that all things shall pass; yet help me to count my blessings of today. Expose me to hate so it not be a stranger; yet fill my cup with love to turn strangers into friends.

But all these things be only if thy will. I am a small and a lonely grape clutching the vine yet thou hast made me different from all others. Verily, there must be a special place for me. Guide me. Help me. Show me the way.

Let me become all you planned for me when my seed was planted and selected by you to sprout in the vineyard of the world.

Help this humble salesman. Guide me, God.

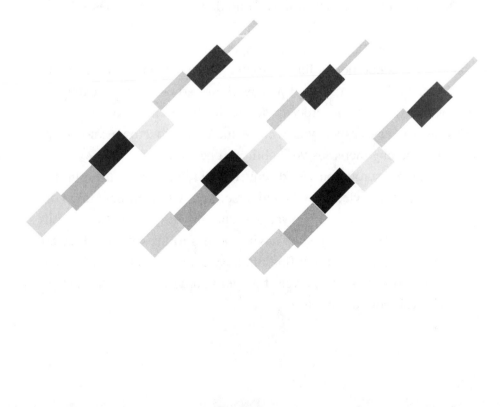

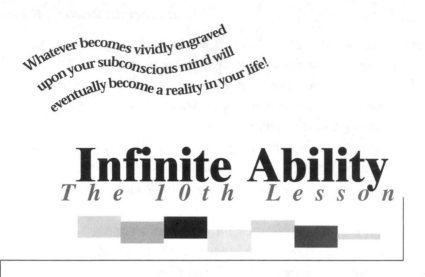

Whatever becomes vividly engraved upon your subconscious mind will eventually become a reality in your life!

Infinite Ability

T h e   1 0 t h   L e s s o n

Your ability to perform is limited by the boundaries of your knowledge. The less knowledge you have about sales, the fewer skills you will have as a salesperson. However, the knowledge you possess is not merely limited to the knowledge inside your mind.

If you work with a team of people, their knowledge is an extension of your knowledge. In order to access it all you need to do is ask a question. Every answer you receive increases your own knowledge base and thereby increases your ability to perform.

In the tenth scroll you will discover how to access the most unlimited source of knowledge in the universe. You will learn how to go on-line through the power of prayer and surf the ultimate net of infinite intelligence. However, just as having access to the Internet does not automatically mean you will find the answers you need; likewise, you must learn how to use the power of prayer in order to locate the answers that will lead you to success.

1| The Instinctive Knowledge of God

"From where has this deep instinct come which escapes from the mouth of all living creatures in moments of peril?"

Most of us have a subconscious awareness that God exists. No matter what name He or She is called, we believe that there is a Supreme Being. We know that we did not create ourselves, yet we are here.

This is not an attempt to influence your religious beliefs or opinion about the nature of God and the responsibility of humanity. When trouble comes suddenly into our lives, many of us automatically call out to God before we fully realize what we are doing. Because humans possess this reflective instinct, then it would appear that we are all aware that God does exist, even if it is only a subconscious awareness.

2| The Nature of Prayer

"Are not our cries a form of prayer?"

A baby cries because he has no words to communicate his request. The older we become, the less our tears are triggered by external physical discomforts. By the time we are adults, our tears flow only when we sense an internal emotional discomfort. Like the infant, we cry, not merely to announce our discomfort, but to seek relief.

By definition, prayer is an intensely earnest request. But to whom do we make our request? When the pain of life causes you to cry out like a whistling teakettle, is it merely to announce the pressure on you or to seek its relief? When your problems seem bigger than you, to whom can you turn to obtain relief?

When we cry for help, it would only be logical that we should direct our cries toward someone who can actually help, someone who can answer prayer.

3 Deciding to Pray
"Henceforth, I will pray,"

Once there was a man who decided that a car was a convenience that should be used only in emergencies. He was seen walking all around town, never taking a cab, bus or any other form of rapid transportation, unless there was an emergency. "If God had intended us to ride he would have given us wheels," was his philosophy. However, the more walking he did, the more emergencies he created. The time he wasted walking made him late for appointments and ultimately forced him to reconsider his decision and take advantage of rapid transportation.

So goes the story of those who wait until an emergency before they decide to pray. If prayer can indeed work in a time of crisis, wouldn't it be wise to use such a helpful tool at those times when no crisis is pending? To wait until your business is going under before you seek the wisdom of a consultant is not a smart business decision. Likewise, to wait until your life is in chaos before using the power of prayer is not a smart life decision.

4 Praying for Guidance
"Only for guidance will I pray, that I may be shown the way to acquire these things,"

People sometimes give up praying after they have prayed for several things that fail to materialize. Such people are not praying, they are merely wishing.

God is not a magician, a genie, or a leprechaun. The process of prayer is nothing like wishing on a star or sending a letter to Santa. The focus of prayer should not be to acquire material things or divine favors, but to seek guidance.

The knowledge of how to accomplish a task is of much greater value than the task completed. Likewise, receiving guidance on how to acquire something is more valuable than the something you acquire. When you know how to do something, you can reproduce the results anytime you desire.

5 | Expecting an Answer
"and my prayers will always be answered."

How would you feel if someone were to call you on the phone, ramble on without letting you speak, then hang up the phone before you ever had a chance to respond? You would feel that it was a rather one sided conversation, wouldn't you? Yet, isn't that exactly what we do when we pray without taking time out to listen for the answer?

But how can we possibly hear from God? What I am about to tell you may not be the only way you can hear the answer to your prayers, but it is one way. As you read these words, think back to the last time you had a good idea. Because it was a fresh idea you suspected it was not one of your own wandering thoughts.

Now, imagine that you prayed for guidance, then sat quietly and listened for the answer. You're not listening for an audible voice, but rather for an idea that will provide the guidance you seek. Whether the idea comes right away or over a period of time, when it pops into your mind, it is the answer to your prayers.

Often, expecting an answer makes it easier for you to recognize it when it comes. If you were not expecting it, the answer could be right under your nose and you would never even notice it.

6 | Give Me This Day My Daily Bread
"Teach me how to hunt with words and prosper with love so that I may be a lion among men and an eagle in the marketplace."

Animals instinctively go about their daily activity of dealing with the challenges required for their survival. Since humans are more intelligent than animals it would seem that they should possess the instinctive skills needed to survive in the concrete jungle of today's marketplace. However, humans are not merely creatures of instinct, they are creatures of reason and intelligent thought. Therefore, it is only fitting that we seek guidance from a Supreme Being because that is the rational thing to do.

In the field of sales, as in any professional field, success often depends on knowing how to use the tools of the trade. To the salesperson, words are one of their most important tools. As the hammer is to the carpenter and the wrench is to the mechanic, so are words to the successful salesperson.

And the unshakable foundation of all true success is love. Love for the work you do and the people you serve gives you the ability to enjoy the satisfaction of success at every stage of your progress regardless of the financial level you ultimately attain. Therefore, seeking guidance in the development of these areas is essential to living a fulfilling life.

7 | Help Me to Endure Opposition
"Help me to remain humble through obstacles and failure,"

A branch that will not bend in the wind will break. Humility gives us the flexibility we need to avoid being broken by oppositions encountered along the pathway to success. Humility makes us flexible by taking the heavy burden of flawless perfection from our shoulders.

When egotistical people achieve success, they refer to themselves as self-made. When egotistical people fail, it is always someone else's fault. The reality is that no one ever succeeds or fails by himself; there are always others involved. The humble person, having accepted this fact is better prepared to deal with whatever comes.

We are creatures with shortcomings and are bound to make mistakes. When a humble person is faced with an obstacle or failure, he takes it in stride and keeps right on going. A humble person can achieve great success without becoming big headed, and can endure a temporary setback without becoming discouraged.

8 | Help Me to Seize Opportunity
"Favor me with alertness to recognize opportunity,"

One person looks at a vacant piece of land in an inner city and sees a rubbish dump. Another looks at the same vacant lot and sees a magnificent skyscraper where business will thrive and citizens will find jobs. The only difference is in the perception of the observer. Just as beauty is in the eye of the beholder, so is opportunity.

The word opportunity means an open port or harbor. To recognize, means that you see something you have seen before. To be able to recognize opportunities when they appear is simply a matter of training your eye. Familiarizing yourself with a variety of opportunities can enhance your ability to spot other opportunities when they pop up.

Praying for the alertness to spot opportunities will help you make greater use of the powers of your imagination.

9 | Help Me to Reach My Full Potential
"Let me become all you planed for me..."

Imagine how different the world would be if we all made better use of our potential. Most computer and software companies provide free customer support for their products. Because of the complex technical nature of these products you need a skilled technician available whom you can call for assistance. By taking advantage of the support service you will probably be able to access more of the product's potential capabilities because you will have help directly from the manufacturer.

Prayer is the only way to access the support services available for the human machine. Through prayer you can obtain help directly from the "manufacturer" and thereby discover how to make greater use of the tremendous untapped potential that you possess.

10 | Help Me Find the Path to Success
"Help this humble salesman. Guide me, God."

Without some assistance it is difficult to find a place you have never been. However, the assistance you receive from others may not always lead you to the destiny you desire. Success means different things to different people. What one person may consider the ultimate success might bring you the ultimate sorrow.

God is the only source of guidance who can show you exactly how to reach your desired destination of success. The real difficulty comes not in obtaining the guidance, but rather in following through on the instructions after they have been received.

If you have never received the guidance you need for a fulfilled life, then stop now and take a moment to pray. Ask God to guide you and then listen calmly for the answer. However, once you have received guidance, it will be up to you to do what is necessary. If you have already received guidance and you know how to reach your desired destination, then just keep on following. If you have gotten off track, start fresh and begin again today. You will eventually reach your destination if you just keep moving in that direction.

A Practical Exercise

The following exercise can help you use the power of prayer in a practical manner. What you are about to do is create your own Self-Fulfilling Prophesy. The first step in the process is to create a clear mental picture of the outcome you desire. To do this, first write out a general description of your future, as you want it to be. Describe what you want your life to look like within the next five to ten years.

1. What are the personal qualities and characteristics you want to possess?
2. What is the professional position and income level you want to achieve?
3. What type of friends and family relationships do you want to have?
4. What will be the condition of your mental and physical health?
5. What is the social standing and impact you want to have in your community?
6. What type of contribution do you want to make for the benefit of humanity?
7. What will be the level of your spiritual and intellectual maturity?

Since this is a sales training program, I have narrowed the focus of the exercise to create an outcome specifically related to increasing your sales profits or personal income. You can use this exercise to create a desired outcome in any area of your life by simply changing its focus.

First: Establish the target for your mental focus (in this case it is increased income).

Second: Gather and digest as much information related to that subject as possible.

Third: Apply this mathematical equation: X+Y=Z or (Z-Y=X) X is the unknown.

"Z" is what you want. It is a vivid description of the desired outcome you want. For this exercise, "Z" should be the dollar amount by which you intend to increase your income.

"Y" is what you have. It is a detailed inventory of all the things that you currently possess, things that can be used to help you achieve the dollar amount stated in "Z."

"X" is what you need. It is an unknown factor and will require you to use your imagination. It is what you can use to bridge the gap between "Y" and "Z."

The clearer you can see "X" in your mind, the easier it will be for you to complete this exercise. Since "X" is something you don't have, avoid the temptation to let your mind limit what it could possibly be. To help you do this, stretch your mind by forcing it to consider even the most far-fetched ideas of what "X" could be. You can always tone down your creative ideas after you have put them on the table. However, you cannot get a clear look at them until you draw them out of your head.

Once you have identified "X," write it down and make it the focus of your prayer request. Pray repeatedly if necessary, but once you get the answer, give thanks and take action.

A Tribute to Og Mandino

Throughout the centuries God has selected special messengers to help translate the words of wisdom to the world. Og Mandino was such a messenger, and his symphony of work still sings aloud within the hearts of millions who were touched by his genius.

During his life Og spent countless hours studying the books of philosophers, prophets, scholars and sages. By digging deep down within the pages of these books he uncovered treasures of truth. Now Og has crossed beyond the boundary of time into the realm of eternity and bequeathed his priceless gems of inspiration. Adorn your mind with these precious jewels and let them beautify your spirit.

Use the ten scrolls as keys to unlock life's mysteries. You will gain access to an unlimited bounty of material riches and emotional fulfillment. You will also realize that the greatest achievement is not acquiring the bounty but discovering the keys. So let your heart rejoice now in your discovery, and celebrate life as if you were already in possession of the abundant success that you seek.

The light of Og's knowledge still radiates with the sun's brilliance. The eternal river of wisdom that flows from the pages of his books will forever refresh those who submerge themselves within its depths. I ask that you join me in this tribute to the late great Og Mandino, by embracing his message and using it to impact your life and your world. For as the poet Kahlil Gibran so appropriately put it: "If you wish to pay him due reverence, assert your claim to a portion of the knowledge in the books of wisdom he has left as a legacy to the world." By doing so we can help to echo that cry of wisdom so that its voice will reach the ears of many generations to come.

Let me leave you with a closing story and prayer, because it epitomizes the most important thing I want you to remember from this training program. The point is this: whatever becomes vividly engraved upon your subconscious mind, will eventually become a reality in your life!

Many years ago, during a time of great financial struggle, I stayed up late one night trying to calculate my bills. No matter how many times I added them up, my expenses continued to exceed my income. Then, just about the time I reached the height of my frustration, the burglar alarm on my car began to sound. I went outside and turned it off, looked around, and saw no one. My car was parked in a wide-open area and if someone had been tampering with it, I would have been able to see him or her. Nevertheless, I put the thought out of my mind and went back in the house, back to crunching my numbers. Within less than 15 minutes, the alarm sounded again. I went back outside and thought, "Maybe God is trying to tell me something." I looked up to the sky, at the millions of stars, and my heart took flight on the wings of my eyes, far out into the vast reaches of the universe. Suddenly my problems seem to shrink to nothing. At that moment, I felt a great sense of peace, and I prayed, "Lord help to capture the essence of this moment permanently in my mind. Help me to remember this peace I feel now whenever worries and anxiety try to overtake me."

Three days later I was inspired to write a poem. I took that poem and engraved it on my subconscious mind so that whenever I became tempted to worry or became tormented with anxiety, I could draw upon the memory of the poem and immediately return my attitude to a state of peace and tranquility. In fact, when problems occur in my life now, this poem is automatically triggered and begins to play in my head like a song, lulling me into a peaceful frame of mind.

I leave you with this poem, because hopefully it will remind you that as you engrave the principles of Og Mandino's ten ancient scrolls on your sub-conscious mind, they will help you maintain the right attitude you need to achieve success. My prayer for you is this:

As you are confronted with the inevitable challenges that you will face in life, may the wisdom of the scrolls be automatically triggered in your mind, and continue to guide you toward your desired destination of success.

Prayer

*So many things you want to do, sometimes your goals
   may seem so far.*
*And yet you strive with all in you, to move on from
   where you are.*
*But when life's burdens come to bear, and no change
   seems to come about,*
*The knees bend easily in Prayer, in hopes that God will
   work it out.*

*Tears fall upon your folded hands, for you have
   nowhere else to turn.*
*And hoping God will understand, your humble heart
   within you yearns.*
*But before you even say a word, your inner voice begins
   to speak.*
*To you it's suddenly occurred, exactly whom it is you
   seek.*

"He is the everlasting King, with whom there is no end.
*The sole creator of all things, He's God and He's your
   friend.*
*The one who made all you can see, He made the earth,
   moon, sun, and sky.*
*And sent IIis Son to set you free, upon the cross for you
   He died.*

*He made the stars that heaven shows, and galaxies far
   out of sight.*
*So what request could you propose, that could intimi-
   date His might?"*
*Upon this thought your fears subside, and your anxi-
   eties all cease.*
*You find yourself engulfed inside, the presence of the
   God of peace.*

*You don't recall a single phrase, of what you thought to
   say.*
*But a troubled prayer now comes out praise, knowing
   that God will make a way.*

Denis Waitley

*D*r. Denis Waitley is recognized as a world authority on high-level achievement and personal excellence. He has been the mental trainer for Apollo astronauts, Superbowl champions and U.S. Olympic teams. With over 10 million of his motivational audio tapes sold in 14 languages, he is the most-listened-to voice on personal and professional development. He is, perhaps, best know as the author/narrator of *The Psychology of Winning,* the all-time best-selling, non-musical program. This tape series has generated nearly $100 million in sales since its initial release in 1978.

Waitley has also authored ten non-fiction books on self-management, including two national bestsellers: *The Seeds of Greatness* and *Being the Best,* and his newest release is *Empires of the Mind.* Dr. Waitley is one of America's most sought after keynote speakers in corporations, associations, and institutions. Recognized as a world authority on high-level achievement and personal excellence, Waitley was named "Outstanding Platform Speaker of the Year" by the Sales and Marketing Executives' Association. He was also recently inducted into the International Speakers' Hall of Fame in St. Louis, Missouri.

Waitley was the founding director of the National Council on Self-

Esteem and the President's Council on Vocational Education, in 1991. He received the "Youth Flame Award" from the National Council on Youth Leadership for his outstanding contribution to high school youth leadership. During the 1980s, Waitley was appointed by William Simon, president of the U.S. Olympic Committee, to serve as the first non-physician on the Committee's Sports Medicine Council. As Chairman of Psychology, he was responsible for creating the mental training program to enhance the performance of all U.S. Olympic athletes. Additionally, Waitley was a visiting scholar at the University of Southern California.

In the 1970s, Waitley served as president of the International Society for Advanced Education, a non-profit foundation inspired by Dr. Jonas Salk and other leading health scientists. He also studied and counseled returning U.S. POWs from Vietnam. While completing his graduate studies, during the 1960s, Waitley served as Consultant to the president of the Salk Institute for Biological Studies in La Jolla, California. Also during this period, he conducted simulation and stress management for NASA's Apollo astronauts. A former Navy pilot, Waitley is a graduate of the U.S. Naval Academy at Annapolis. He received his Ph.D. in human behavior from La Jolla University in 1979. He and his wife, Susan, reside in Rancho Santa Fe, California. They have seven adult children.

! • | Discovering the Secrets of the Successful

How did you get started in the field of sales?

I have never been directly in sales but have always been in the field of persuasion, perception and self-development. Everyone is a sales executive, especially today. My belief is: "You only sell you. The decision of the buyer is based on the value of the seller. Just as products have a brand recognition, so do individuals. A "personal brand" is determined by the integrity, reliability, creativity and value of the service offered.

What is the greatest challenge you have had to face over the years?

The greatest challenges I have had to overcome in my life were the low self-esteem from having been raised in a low income, dysfunctional family, and later, in life, winning a battle over cancer.

What do you consider to be the most outstanding achievement of your career?

The most outstanding achievement of my career has been to be a role model worthy of emulation by my six children and by the next generation.

Who were some of you most influential role models and mentors?

The three most influential role models in my life have been my grandmother, who encouraged me to read and plant *The Seeds of Greatness* in my mind; Dr. Jonas Salk, the developer of the first polio vaccine, who encouraged me to gain a doctorate in human behavior and inspired me to seek answers to life and health instead of disease and cure, and Dr. Viktor Frankl, Holocaust survivor and author of *Man's Search for Meaning,* who as my professor suggested that we petition for a Statue of Liberty in New York.

What is the most effective sales technique you have ever used?

The only sales technique I use is to help the other person solve his or her problems or help him or her achieve a major goal, need to desire, through my efforts. I believe in giving more in service than I expect to receive in payment, which creates motivation and trust in the other person.

Give an example of how you would apply this technique in a real life situation?

In real life, I ask questions and listen. By paying attention and value to the other person, I immediately signal to that person that I place his or her interests above my own. I go into every relationship expecting to give first and contribute first, before it is clear that I will receive something in return. What I silently say to myself is. "I'll make them glad they talked to me today." What I hope they silently think to themselves is " I like me best when I'm with him."

What is the most valuable advice you can offer an aspiring sales person?

Make certain your are totally committed to and believe in your product or service. Know its features and limitations. Don't jut try to close the sale. Open you a long-term relationship by putting the needs and desires of your prospect above your needs and desires to earn money.

If you have not always lived by your current philosophy, what provoked the change?

At one point in my life I became impressed with the acquisition of material achievements as a measure of my success. The change occurred when I realized that no one cares what you have accomplished, unless it benefits them and their dreams.

O n   O g   M a n d i n o ' s
Ten Ancient Scrolls
Denis Waitley

W hen I first noticed Og Mandino, I had not read his books. He was heading up W. Clement Stone's little TV guide-sized Success Magazine. What caught my attention was that he had the most unusual, interesting name I had even seen. Og reminded me of the many books I had read about our earliest ancestors. Mandino reminded me of an unfettered spirit that could not be harnessed. How wonderfully appropriate this name, Og Mandino, for a man whose creativity and legacy will live forever.

He had the wisdom of the ages, combined with an original gift for allegorical inspiration that enfolded the reader as the main character in each of his masterpieces. To me, each of his literary contributions is a rare gemstone, my Mandino library is full, from *The Greatest Salesman in the World*, which I keep next to my first copy of the Bible, to The Twelfth Angel, and Ten Ancient Scrolls for Success.

I could articulate a full term-paper expressing my unashamed awe and respect for his contribution to the human potential movement. Suffice to say that Russell Conwell, James Allen, Abraham Maslow, Carl Rogers, Earl Nightingale and Norman Vincent Peale may not, in concert, have influenced as many lives as Og Mandino. He, of the written word, is like my friend Billy Graham, of the spoken word. Different in so many ways, they both are without peer in delivering a passionate belief that transcends language, culture and time.

If imitation is the height of flattery, then Og is at the summit. His style has been copied generously during the past three decades. Several clones have become national best sellers. None in my opinion, has had the depth or brilliance of an authentic Mandino work of art. There should be a Mandino Institute for Original Inspiration. Today, I fear, books to warm the heart and lift the fallen are produced rather than written. It is tempting and all too easy to assemble a collection of other people's favorite stories than pay the price of genius, which requires years and hours of effort and research.

Backstage, at the Positive Thinking Rallies, it was a rare treat just to sit and share a yarn with Og during the 1970s and 80s. While Paul Harvey, Art Linkletter, Zig Ziglar, Robert Schuller and Norman Vincent Peale were performing, Og would look me square in the eyes and ask a hundred questions about my career, my writing, my speaking, my desires...my life. Yet, his own life was somewhat mysterious to me.

And different. When I first shared the platform with Og, I thought the electricity had failed due to a storm in the Chicago area, I looked between the curtains on the stage and saw a candle burning on the podium. I knew the power was definitely out! Then, in that resonant, confident tone, I heard the voice Og Mandino booming through the speakers to affirm The Ten Ancient Scrolls for Success. I hadn't experienced anything quite like that since I first saw Charleston Heston's hair and beard turn white while receiving The Ten Commandments! There is only one Og Mandino. And the mold has been broken.

I could almost hear him speaking to me recently as I walked through my orchard, on a hill near the sea. "Today I begin a new life. And I make a solemn oath to myself that nothing will retard my new life's growth. . . Much has been filtered and tossed to the wind. Only the pure truth lies distilled in the words to come. I will drink as instructed and spill not a drop. And the seed of success I will swallow. Today, my old skin has become dust. I will walk tall among men and they will know me not, for today I am a new man, with a new life." You are indeed, a new man, Og—our beloved friend—and because of the imprint of your ballads, "I will greet this day with love in my heart."